The Grand Union Canal and its

● Left:

Course of [illegible] Canal fron[illegible] Birmingha[illegible] the Midland network of waterways, showing also its junction with the River Trent giving access to the North Eastern network.

N

0 20
Miles

● Below:

Plan showing course of canal through London to Regents Canal Dock and Brentford Basin. The fitting-out, fuelling and repair depôt was opposite Bull's Bridge.

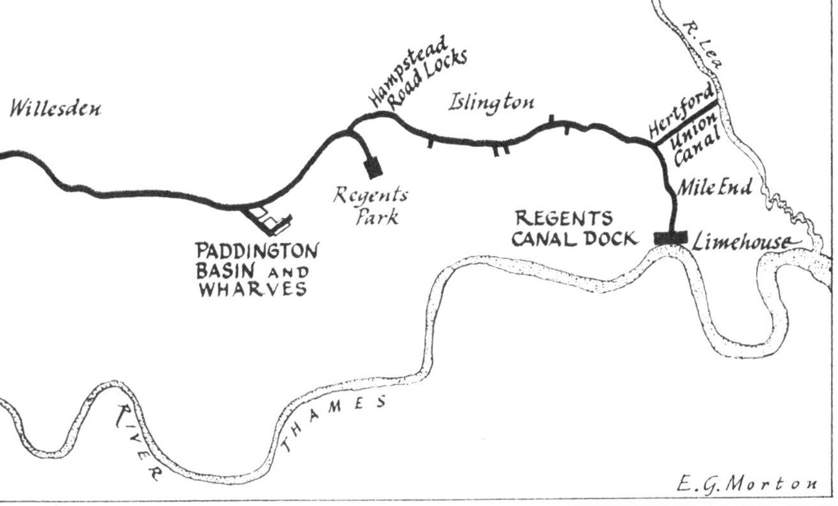

Hold on a Minute

Hold on a Minute

BY

TIM WILKINSON

B

M & M BALDWIN
Cleobury Mortimer, Salop
1990

BIBLIOGRAPHIC NOTE

This book was first published by George Allen & Unwin Ltd in 1965. A second edition was issued in 1970, with a new 'Author's Note' dated February 1970. Some sheets of the second edition were bound up into paperback form and issued by Waterway Productions Ltd.

The text, illustrations, and endpaper maps of the first edition are here reproduced with a few corrections, together with the 'Author's Note' from the second edition. The bibliography has been omitted, but this new edition has a new Foreword by Sonia Rolt, and an index. The publishers are grateful to Unwin Hyman Ltd for their co-operation.

ISBN 0 947712 14 3

Published by M & M Baldwin
24 High Street, Cleobury Mortimer
Kidderminster, Worcs DY14 8BY

Printed by The Redwood Press Ltd
Pegasus Way, Bowerhill
Melksham, Wilts SN12 6TR

FOR

P.S.W.

ACKNOWLEDGEMENTS

I wish to thank Mr Hugh McKnight of Upper Halliford, Shepperton-on-Thames, for permission to reproduce the photograph of narrow boats used on the jacket, also those in plates numbers 2(a), 2(b), 3(a), 4(b), 5(a), 5(b), 6(a), 8(a), and Mr G. A. Oliver of Glasgow for those in plates numbers 1(a) and 7(b).

FOREWORD TO THE THIRD EDITION

When Tom Rolt wrote his Foreword to the first edition of this book, fourteen years had passed since he had left the canals. He shared with the author the experience of the canals as they had been a couple of decades earlier, so both men had a perspective on the life which only time could provide.

It cannot be said that they looked back to canals in their heyday. Who, indeed, can say when such a heyday was? Could it have been in the time before railway competition killed off contracts and left half of canal life moribund or in a fluctuating decline? Could it have been at the height of the family boats or when the Number Ones predominated, before they were superseded by carrying companies, large and small? Tom Rolt in the chapter on the working boatman in his book *The Inland Waterways of England* made the case for the Number Ones as the highest epitome of craft, landscape, work and people.

Tim Wilkinson and his wife moved onto their boats 'Chiswick' and 'Bawtry' too late to see the Number Ones in their full diversity, but met them, and some of the best of their families, in their new role working boats for the Grand Union Canal Carrying Company, Samuel Barlow Coal Carrying Company, and S E Barlow, amongst others.

It was the encounter with the canal community as well as a sharp and sensitive reaction to the beguiling landscape of reflecting waters, functional artifacts, bridges and buildings, as well as the darker aspects of ruined or toppling industry in carious stretches of poisoned waters, which the two men had in common. It made Tom Rolt an admirer of the courage and high spirits of the Wilkinsons in their will to make a success of running a pair of working narrow boats and, later, a supporter and helper to Tim Wilkinson in the publication of his book – this book, which describes so graphically their brief but intense encounter with the world of the Cut.

I have a copy of the first edition, which I treasure since it is inscribed to Tom Rolt and myself with kind words from the author. It was therefore with some trepidation, as well as feeling it a touching honour, that I received a request from the publishers to write a new foreword to the present edition. In recent years, M & M Baldwin have done great service to the memory of the last years of narrow-boat carrying by publishing new editions of several books about working boats in the 1940s.

It was the tolerantly held belief among the working boat community that without actually living the life it was not possible to describe the working ways and the feeling of this life passed in work and movement. It is exactly this quality of which Tim Wilkinson's book is so splendidly full.

Craft and trade memories are precious, and quite rare. It is only comparatively recently that efforts, some successful, have been made to capture in oral history practices long ceased or ceasing.

It is the way Tim Wilkinson found to describe canal working practice of the time, and his wonder and absorption it it, while modestly recording his own initial ignorance, which makes the book so valuable. With more impatience he describes bureaucratic hold-ups, delays relating to cargoes, inefficient loading and unloading methods, and the notorious state of some parts of the canal system. It was finally a combination of these factors, and the harshness of the life, which drove him to abandon hopes of sustaining such a life, both economically and physically.

The book is graphic and truthful, the best of reporting. Few people have come 'off the land' to work canal boats, and even fewer have been able to describe the life as well as Tim Wilkinson. It is this which makes his book, as far as I know, unique; the only other book of this type is Eily Gayford's *The Amateur Boatwomen*, her account of taking to the canals during the second World War. She is reticent about the boaters, and Wilkinson philosophises to some degree, as did Tom Rolt, when confronted by these nomads, who are so clever at doing what they do (or did) and whose lives added up to some total and satisfying experience for the perceptive onlooker or engaged imitator. It is possible to use the modern term 'holistic' in relation to this life, though the Wilkinsons or any other boaters would be amazed to hear it applied to themselves.

But while the first changes from mainly commercial to partial pleasure use were taking place on the canals another tendency was starting – and continues to grow. It pays more respect, not less, to the world described by Tim Wilkinson and Tom Rolt, as that world slips inexorably into the past. It is shown by the periodic if small-scale attempts to trade, by the vigour of the pleasure-boat movement in more authentic craft, by the desire of people to possess a true narrow boat, to decorate it authentically, and to travel and experience the canals in a knowledgeable way.

Following this, and with much urging and lobbying from the Inland Waterways Association and others, Government, in the shape of the British Waterways Board, becomes aware of the need to authenticate the threatened canal landscape. Pubs are revived, moorings developed, warehouses and drydocks saved. A secondary patination comes into existence. Shrubs and bedding plants do not go particularly well with engineering brick so it is not always successful. But Heritage attends, and is likely to remain, albeit challenged in places by dominating development which may dwarf and destroy such small human assemblages as much as neglect can. The tramping boots, the scouring ropes and grit are gone. The secret countryside leaching into cities along these waters is largely tidied up.

Tim Wilkinson's book revives a time when this life survived. In the foreground of his landscape, firmly placed, are the boatman and woman, their quality as he found it and as it changed him.

It is a salutary tale.

SONIA ROLT

22 January 1990

AUTHOR'S NOTE

When writing the Foreword to *Hold on a Minute* in 1965, Mr L. T. C. Rolt suggested that it would soon be a valuable historic document. It has, I am happy to say, become a widely read and valued record of a unique but small, colourful and persistently interesting social group that has almost completely faded away —the boaters of England's canals; the strange people off the cuts who lived, worked and died in their traditionally painted narrow boats.

That they strove to persist in an old, largely unchanged manner of life to preserve their customs, beliefs and superstitions far in the twentieth century was more than anachronistic, it was indicative both of a deep attachment to the nature and style of their generally inherited calling, and the width of the crevasse which eventually divided them from their contemporaries 'on the land'. No lesser reasons could have explained either their continued willingness to live under the conditions they did, or their acceptance to the end of such meagre repayment as was doled out to them for their skilful, often dangerous, always arduous work.

Although the traditional boaters and working narrow boats are gone from Britain's rivers, navigations and canals, there are today more boats, more men, women and children, using and enjoying the beauty and quiet of what remains of our inland waterways than at any time in their long and interesting histories. These wise and happy modern boaters seen here—along some still pond where herons fish, coots and moor hens scurry—an empty lay-by, a winding hole, a staircase; there, a pumping house, a cut-side inn and shop all in one; everywhere, solid evidence of a busy, engaging past. What went on in those days? How did the boaters live, work, raise families in those tiny cabins? What was a cratch, a dipper, breasting-up, a Josher? What were straps, snubbers and snatchers? The answers to these and numerous other questions are found in this book.

Following its original publication I was pleased to receive a few small and mispelled and many long hand- and type-written letters of thanks for—and appreciation of—*Hold on a Minute*. They came not only from Britain but from divers distant countries, and have, together with orders for further copies, continued to arrive. Because of the ceaseless demand for this book—long since out of print—the fast growing interest in, and use of, the inland waterways for holiday and recreational purposes, the need for a new impression of it became evident. That this should reappear in a year dedicated to conservancy is apt.

Our inland waterways, and much of the land bordering them, remain the undisturbed haunts of countless animals. Those who have long cherished these, and the many who may come to hold a like persuasion, may wonder how they can contribute to the essential alertness and, as is frequently necessary, the battle to preserve the rich and mostly beautiful heritage of Britain's waterways. The answer, clearly, is to join that body which has for so many years fought for this cause and numerous others associated with it. Under the aegis of the Inland Waterways Association (114, Regents Park Road, London, N.W.1.) lies strength; in it rests the one great hope for the future preservation of our rivers, canals and navigations, and the effective conservation of the wild life near and in them.

TIM WILKINSON

February, 1970

FOREWORD

L. T. C. ROLT

All over the canal system disused wharves are acquiring a new lease of life as mooring stations for holiday cruisers. This is a result of the wide recognition of their amenity value which our canals have won during the last decade or so. This activity is to be welcomed because the alternative was stagnation and decay. Yet those of us who have known the canals for many years must inevitably lament the passing of their old workaday life—the life of the narrow boats—which has ebbed so rapidly away in the last twenty years.

The disappearance of the bravely painted and burnished narrow boat with its nomadic family will soon make this book a valuable historic document, for this is the life that Mr Wilkinson describes, not as a mere bystander on the towpath but at first-hand as the captain of such a boat. Posterity is bound to be grateful to him for electing to go canal boating the hard way and for recording so perceptively and graphically an experience that can never be repeated.

It was no romantic idyll; Mr Wilkinson soon discovered what it takes to keep a pair of boats on the move in all weathers. The job was tough, so tough that it was bound to become an anachronism in our push-button welfare state, something for economist and sociologist alike to shake their heads over. Yet it was the way of life of a people whose like we shall not see again, a people whose qualities belong to an older England, illiterate but wise, poor yet proud. That is why those of us who, like the writer of this book, were privileged to know the boaters must find the canals the poorer for their passing.

CONTENTS

ILLUSTRATIONS

between pages 64 and 65

PART ONE

Winter

CHAPTER I

A Chance Meeting at Fishery Inn

It is interesting to consider how snap decisions, chance meetings, have affected the course of one's life.

I was motoring down the A.41 towards London and home at Richmond, thinking all the way; thinking how tired I was of driving, how dissatisfied with my life, how dearly I should like, once again, to be doing something useful. Those first few years after the end of the war had been interesting, exciting, creative. I had searched the country for empty buildings which would convert to factories, altered them, installed machinery to give the most efficient production, gathered teams of workers, trained them, tuned them to the machines and tuned the machines also.

Directors welcomed me then. I was a great fellow, a wonderful chap. Of course, they could do nothing without me. They knew nothing of these tasks, had no experience of running factories, no understanding of machines, but they had—money.

As soon as their mounts were found and trained, and they were assisted into the saddle, off they went. As with children shown how to work a new toy, their demand was to be left alone to play. But they failed. The toy ceased to work, and up went wails, 'Come, come quickly. I have fallen,' or, 'It won't work. It's gone wrong. Oh please make it go again.' Once more I was in demand.

But the day soon came when they learned how to get along without assistance. Then it was that my chief ordered me to keep an eye on them, whether they liked it or not. 'Our products must be homogeneous. Your job now is to make quite sure that no one fiddles with the formulae or introduces his own notions. Their agreements with this, the parent company, give me the right at all times to check and test their output. You are my representative and technical director, and you will do just that. To the devil with their likes and dislikes.'

So it was that I began motoring round the country, dropping in here and there; unexpected, uninvited and—resented. For this 'work' they paid me well, but because of it I felt like a spiv.

Then there was the problem of 'home'. We had one room in a small house in which four branches of a family lived. This was post-war England! Even there we were not safe, and every effort, trick and pressure was being used to get us out. There were four wives in one kitchen. Other people's children, screaming babies, surrounded us. Yes, I was a spiv without a home.

I came to Berkhamsted, where I had grown up. Down there were my beloved canal and the station; there the school where I was taught to sing 'Jerusalem', to sing about 'England's green and pleasant land'. 'Have a break,' I thought. 'Pack it in for a while.'

Then I noticed a sign which read 'Boxmoor'. Here Gay and I had found a grand little pub alongside the canal, only just off the main road but in the country, in peace. I had brought her to Berkhamsted to show her where her husband had lived as a child — the houses, the large pipe in the canal where I had learned to fish minnows, the stretch where my model yacht had been wrecked.

Yes this was it—'Fishery Inn'. I drew up, climbed stiffly from the car and walked in.

* * * *

It was a July evening in 1948. Now, years later, I remember it all clearly. The landlord and I had a chat while he pulled my pint. I looked round the room. A short, frail man in rough clothes with some kind of metal handle protruding from the collar of his coat stood with his back to me, looking through the large open window of the bar towards the silver strip of water outside. The metal thing intrigued me. I eased nearer to find out what it was. That did it. He swung round. He had blue eyes. He caught me staring and in a moment we were talking. Later we were deep in excited conversation. Later still we were sitting on the gunwales of his narrow boat, one of us either side of a long upturned wooden tiller, swinging our pint tankards on our fingers. They were both empty, but it did not matter, for we were talking too eagerly to think about drink.

His name was Bishop. He was a happy contented man because

he loved the unusual life he was living. The two boats were his. 'A pair' he called them. The one which we sat on was a 'butty' boat. It had no engine, but was always towed by the other, which was powered by a twin diesel engine housed in a compartment for'ard of the cabin. This was called a 'monkey' boat or motor-boat. Each was 70 feet long by 7 feet beam. Each had a small cabin immediately ahead of the steering position, and for greater comfort he had built an extra cabin on the monkey, for-ard of the engine room.

With him were his wife and son. The three of them worked the 'pair' in cargo sub-contracting to the South Eastern Division of the Docks and Inland Waterways Executive.

They cooked on neat, efficient, miniature coal-ranges, one in each of the aft cabins. Water was carried in large cans. There was electric light, for the engine drove a generator. Storage batteries were carried and put on charge when low.

The average load for a pair was 50 tons of cargo. Going along gently, he earned £18 - £20 a week. If he pushed things hard, this could be raised to £30 - £35 with luck—and a goodly sprinkling of short trips. As boaters—'Not bargees, mind'; he laid great emphasis on this—they had extra rations, including tinned milk off points. When he carried grain in bulk, the 'sweepings' went to farmers. As he said this he winked at me, I smiled but hadn't a clue of the joke.

Expenses were small. The diesel oil he bought from the depôt for a shilling a gallon, and the engine ran, towing the butty, with both loaded, for approximately three-quarters of an hour on a gallon. Coal for the ranges was carried in bunkers in the back end of the holds against the cabin bulkheads. The family didn't buy it. It was a common cargo, and there was an unwritten law that boaters bunkered up from their holds when they were loaded with the best type suitable for their stoves.

A crew of three was better, but frequently he ran his 'pair' two-handed. At the start he had employed an old, widely-experienced boater called Herbert Chitty to teach them the ropes generally and show them around the 'road'.

'The road?' I queried.

'Oh, that's a boater's term. They have a great many—almost their own language. The road is the route generally, and particularly the section of "cut" ahead. "Cut" is canal, and no boater ever refers to it otherwise. On the cut the road can be bad, which might mean that the pounds, or lengths between locks, were short of water, or that there was a pair of boats ahead going in the same direction—in which case all the locks would be against one.'

'I see. Then a good road would be straight, with plenty of water. It would be free of locks, or one along which a pair had come towards one, so that the gates would be open and one could, so to speak, drive right in.'

'You've got it. Now this is where you really need a third hand. On a bad road, he rides along on a bicycle, and sets the locks for his approaching pair.'

'Ah. Now tell me. How do you work when there are only two of you?'

'Then you "breast-up", which means throttling back the monkey to a slow speed before you reach the locks. Up alongside comes the butty. You gather the tow-line, sling it on the bows of the butty—neatly mind; you don't want any knots in it—leaving the looped end handy so that you can grab it easily later. Up she rides, and along to her bows runs her steerer. As the boats come head alongside head, this steerer tosses a strap over the T stud on the monkey boat, and makes it fast to the butty. The boats are now close together, side by side, and the monkey steerer straps up aft also. Now both boats can be controlled by the steerer of the powered one. Simple, eh?'

'Sounds like a neat manoeuvre. Is it difficult?'

'Cor, dear me. The mess you can make of it is amazing! But to finish. You now ease up to the lock, and one of the crew jumps ashore, runs up the stairs and opens the paddles.'

'These "straps", what are they?'

'Straps are ropes. That's all. You have various lengths of rope for different jobs—side straps, cross straps, uphill straps, downhill straps.'

'It's pretty obvious then that a deal of time is wasted in two-handed boats. Can one really make a living with only two?'

'Oh bless you, yes. Plenty of the boaters go two-handed. I've done it myself for many trips and rather like it. The lock work makes a change, and the time wasted is nothing compared with waiting around to be loaded or unloaded.'

'Is there plenty of cargo to share out?'

'All the cargo in the world. In fact, they can't get sufficient pairs crewed. They're running a training scheme now in an attempt to get more boats working.'

'Where do you keep your boats when you are not in cargo? Do you have a base? How do you make contact?'

'Well, as I'm working for the D. & I.W.E., my base is the depôt at Southall—Bull's Bridge. Everything is handled from there, and, what's more, no charges are made. All we pay is a small toll for lock usage, and this is deducted from our cheques.'

'This all sounds almost too easy. What's the snag?'

'I haven't found any snags. Mind you, it's not everybody's idea of how to live, but we are happy. We love it. Why are you so interested?'

I told him just how I was feeling about my life; that both Gay, my wife, and myself had grown up 'messing about in boats', that we had lived on a converted butty boat immediately after my demobilization, and that we loved and were experienced in handling different types of craft—under power and in sail.

'You're a couple of naturals, I should think. The sooner people like you get started the better. Why not drop in at Bull's Bridge and discuss the idea with them? They might even sell you a pair if you want to be a Number One.'

'A Number One? What's that?'

'Oh, simply an owner of his boats. A pair has two steerers, and one is the captain. If the captain also owns the boats, he becomes a Number One.'

'Another question, Mr Bishop. What's this thing in your collar?'

He drew the metal object out, and immediately I remembered —a windlass, the L-shaped metal crank used to wind the gears on the paddles.

We went all over both his boats, exchanged addresses and shook hands. 'Goodbye and good luck, and I hope we meet again —on the cut.' He stood and waved.

I returned to the car and drove slowly towards Richmond, thinking, planning, wondering if I could talk Gay into the idea. For here, it seemed to me, was an exciting and worthwhile solution to both my problems. I remembered how, when I was a child, the towpath had fascinated me. I had cadged lifts, talked to the boaters and shoved the great balance beams for them as they worked up and down through 'Berko' as they called it. A lonely child, I was always dreaming of going beyond that place, up the cut to the great cities for which the cargoes were destined, or, better still, down, right down, to where, so the boaters said, the cut joined a great river which flowed right through London and to the sea.

I was seven years old at that time. I loved the cut. The people were different; the children worked. And then there were the horses—silent, vast, their faces in brown string bags. They were good-tempered, understanding, gentle, but so powerful! I watched them leaning forwards taking the first strain on the tautening, curved tow-line. Out squeezed water, and down along the curve ran sunfilled balls, chasing one another until the first fell gaily into the cut, and all the others followed. I heard again the warning crack of whips, the throbbing of the first diesels, sounds of falling paddles and rising pawls, of windlasses dropped on stone.

By the canal at Berkhamsted my love of boats and ships was born, with my love of water, sailing and fishing. From the canal we moved to a house by the Thames, and there my love grew. In 1945 Gay and I read Mr L. T. C. Rolt's *Narrow Boat*. We enjoyed the book, and decided ourselves to convert and live in a narrow boat. In Brentford Dock we found 'Queen', a wooden butty. We bought her, had her towed to Kingston, and made our home in her during my demobilization leave. Then my first post-war job was secured — at Fordingbridge, on the non-navigable river Avon. 'Queen' was sold. Nine months later the firm moved to London, and we were back again in one room, in the house at Richmond.

* * * *

'You're late. You've been drinking. Come and eat your supper.'

'All right. But you must sit down too. I've something interesting to tell you. Exciting. I've got a plan.'

'What again, Jimmy? What's it this time?'

'How do you like the sound of "James Fern and Wife, Carriers"?'

'I don't.'

'Ah, but let us now add, "By Water". What then?'

'Well, it would be an improvement if you mean in boats. Stop the riddles. What are you talking about?'

'You remember that little pub by the canal in Boxmoor—the one we found by accident?'

'Oh yes. That was a beautiful evening.'

'Well, I've just come from there; just left a man called Albert Bishop, a fellow older than I. Well, he owns . . . '

I talked and talked. She listened and listened. We talked; we argued; we began to make plans.

CHAPTER II

Training and Fitting Out

In the same month we called on the manager of the Grand Union depôt at Southall and the traffic manager in the Port of London Building, Seething Lane. In August we had some correspondence, and finally met officers of the Docks and Inland Waterways Executive at Ruislip. They seemed to welcome us, but, in September, came a letter saying that the Executive had decided that they could not sell us a pair of boats.

This was a blow. Then Gay had a brainwave. 'Perhaps they might hire us a pair at a reasonable rate. It would be worth asking.'

'But the cabin, the extra cabin? They'll never let us build on to their boats.'

'I don't know. Why not? If we pay to have it done, they don't stand to lose anything. You know, I'm not so sure this isn't a brilliant scheme.'

'What's brilliant about it? I'd rather own our boats.'

'Maybe, Jimmy. But I've been thinking about your damaged neck and arm. What if they don't stand the exertion? You remember what the doctor at Roehampton said.'

'Oh yes. But frankly, Gay, if one did all that the medical boys said, one would just give up and rot.'

'The point is this: with rented boats, if anything goes wrong, all one has to do is to quit. I suggest we write again to the Divisional Waterways Officer, make our suggestions, and see if he can persuade the Executive to agree.'

On September 25th we had what was forever afterwards called 'The Great Meeting'. Our plans were approved. A nine-feet-long extra cabin was to be built on a butty boat—not on the monkey as with Bishop. On Bishop's monkey, with two cabins and an engine room, there was hardly any hold left for cargo.

We were to avail ourselves of the training scheme, as and

when we wished. We were to insure the boats, and pay for the cabin and any other extras, but the pair were to be handed over to us complete in every detail. All this was at a nominal rental.

We decided during that meeting that the Divisional Waterways Officer was a grand fellow, and we never had cause to change this opinion. In fact, we became staunch friends. He visited our boats during our career, took a kindly interest in our progress, and did all possible to help and encourage us.

Early in October I left my job in London. We sold everything we possessed which could not be housed or used on the boats. Finally we moved with boxes and cases to my father's house at Hampton-on-Thames, where we would be nearer to Southall. Generously he lent us his car, and daily we motored to different sections of the Grand Union Canal. We walked miles examining flights of locks, memorising the road, and bribing steerers to give us lifts during which we studied their various methods of working.

Our first day of training was exciting, and was spent on a study of the engine and the fittings of the boats. The next day we were to join Herbert Chitty and his mate, who already had a couple of trainees aboard, at noon, at Lock 63. The fellow in charge, one Adams, announced to my considerable surprise that Lock 63 was called Fishery Inn, and was near Boxmoor Railway Station. Strange coincidences. Chitty trained Bishop. I met Bishop at Fishery Inn.

Gay and I arrived there at 11 a.m. Adams turned up at 11.55. Soon a pair of boats came, but they were not Chitty's. We asked about him, and the steerer said he was ahead. Another pair arrived and confirmed this. Adams was livid. We three hopped on a bus and rejoined the cut below Boxmoor. A pair were coming up from London side. Adams asked if they had seen Chitty. They had not, but they were his sons. We boarded their pair, and started working up the locks towards Boxmoor, Gay and I helping, asking questions, and watching every move. We passed five or six locks, and still there was no Chitty. Then we passed the first pair we had seen at Fishery. They said Chitty was at Lock 62, and had been waiting five hours for us. Adams was indignant, and left us to go by road to 62 and tear a strip off Chitty. We continued with the sons, and at the very next lock met Chitty, but no Adams. Chitty was livid, and expressed himself in plain language. The trainees were also livid. Five hours waiting at Boxmoor! What kind of nuisances were we?

We tried to explain how Adams had stated that Lock 63 was the meeting place. It was no fault of ours, but black looks were thrown at us. Herbert Chitty eventually calmed down after giving his opinion of Adams and the two trainees already with him. They were 'Lazy cissies, good for nothing lay-abouts, useless'. The other steerers, he told us, were 'getting' at him. They said he shouldn't train; shouldn't even have a pair of boats. He wanted to give up the task.

The trainees sprawled about as if on holiday on the Broads, doing nothing. They looked tired, dirty and not keen. We felt sorry for Herbert, and worked hard to try to cheer him a little. I stayed on the motor-boat with him; Gay on the butty with his mate. He began to talk to me about the job. He was a good instructor and master steerer. His accuracy, breasted-up through bridge holes was wonderful. Not a touch, and only a few inches to spare on either side. Lovely!

He explained particular little ways of caring for one's boats. One had covers here, covers there, safeguards for paintwork. You took care where you left your windlass, where you stepped and how. We were locking downhill. 'Remember sills and rudders. Remember to make sure the top paddles are down before you draw the others.' We were locking down quickly, trying to beat the oncoming darkness. Herbert Chitty was cheerful again.

We learned much, and he obviously liked teaching people who would listen and try to understand. In darkness we pulled in and moored by 'Iron Bridge', Lock 77, Watford. We said goodbye and thanked him. One of the trainees turned his back on us. The other was already down in the cabin.

Five days later we arose at 6.15 a.m. on a bitterly cold, frosty morning, and made our way to Paddington Bar to meet Chitty at 9 a.m. Above the cut drifted a thick mist. Visibility was bad, and he arrived one-and-a-half hours late. We jumped aboard, and started the journey down the canal through London to Charrington's Barge and Boat Repairing Yard near the Mile End Road, just short of Regent's Canal Dock and the Thames at Limehouse.

The going was difficult, with visibility about two lengths or

140 feet. Soon we came to Maida Hill Tunnel. We had read about these tunnels and the horrors of boating through them, and were interested at undergoing this first experience. Though only 272 yards long, Maida came up to our expectations. Our headlight produced a dispersed beam which pointed to the roof. Diesel fumes, pumped from our vertical exhaust pipe, struck the roof of the tunnel and rebounded into our eyes, bringing down also small particules of soot and dry crumbling mortar. The noise was painful, but ahead was a small round hole, which grew swiftly as we neared the exit.

We passed through this, under Edgware Road and into Regent's Park, where the mist was thicker and visibility down to a length. Chitty taught us to listen for the horns of approaching boats, and the whip-cracking of men leading horses, which drew barges along this section of canal. So to Hampstead Road Lock, Camden Town and Islington's 960-yard tunnel.

We learnt something of why boaters dislike bargees. These heavy-weight semi-landlubbers pulled out right into our course, made passing as difficult as possible, moored their craft at the entrances to bridge-holes and sloped into cafés or pubs, leaving their barges to swing right across and block the cut.

At Charrington's we handed over our butty, and Chitty gave us a lesson in 'winding', or turning round the motor-boat. We watched as he prodded with his boat-hook to the bottom of the cut down aft of the propeller, making certain there was depth enough to turn without fouling the blade or rudder, while we held her bows hard against the far bank. Then we travelled back to Paddington, where we arrived in darkness. He offered to put us ashore, saying, 'It's fourteen miles to the depôt at Bull's Bridge and no locks. You'll get bitter cold.' We wanted to learn all we could before we had our own boats, and it seemed unkind to leave the old man to do this long lap alone. So we decided to keep him company.

Herbert Chitty smiled. He opened the throttle, rested his left forearm on the top of the cabin, and his right hand behind him on the tiller, leant forwards, peered into the blackness 70 feet ahead, and watched his bows. The twisting line of cut now seemed to rush towards us and pass by while the boat remained still. He was quiet, intent, full of care. We were amazed at his keen eyesight, and the precision of his steering. It was now bitterly cold, pitch dark, and still misty, but the grand old man forged ahead, and we arrived in the lay-by at 8.55 p.m. after ten-and-a-half hours' boating under bad conditions. We were frozen almost stiff, tired and much wiser.

A few days later two of the trainees retired. Before leaving, one of them told me that he had quite enjoyed his week's holiday at Government expense with a fiver thrown in, but he really had no interest in the waterways. They had no future. There was no money in them, and precious little to learn, and it was 'dead easy'. The third left on the following day because he wanted to see his wife. So the great training scheme came to a halt, and we were left to gain experience any way we might. We spent November walking the towpaths, watching, helping, and hanging around Brentford Dock, where there was much activity and plenty to learn.

Early in December a message came that our butty was ready, complete with extra cabin, built-in chest of drawers, a wide shelf down each side for books, and a strong slatted framework athwart ships along the bulkhead to the hold. On this we planned to place a really good spring mattress. We could move aboard as soon as we liked, and push on with the task of fitting her out with all the gear, which would be issued from the stores. The motor-boat was nearly ready, and must, of course, also be equipped. As soon as these tasks were completed, we should inform the office, and our name would go on the list of pairs awaiting a cargo.

* * * *

We overloaded our borrowed car with clothes, provisions, cutlery, crocks, books, oil lamps, torches, tools, and 'the kettle'—'*The* kettle', not just a kettle. This was extra large, and superior in shape, gauge and stability. It stood firm and still on top of the small range, singing quietly, steam curling from its spout, day in day out until finally we left the cut.

Slowly we headed for the depôt, drove the car as near to the water as possible, and then hurried to the lay-by. We spotted her immediately. With new paint and extra cabin, she stood out from all others. Like them she was moored stern to the quay. Near, and looking at her, stood a small group of boaters chatting and pointing. As we approached, the bunch broke, and nobody acknowledged our cheerful greeting. We dumped our loads, and gazed, feeling all at the same time excited, proud, happy and not a little terrified by her seeming vastness. Could we handle two such boats loaded with 50 tons of cargo? Was it possible to steer such a lengthy craft around some of the corners we had seen on our towpath walks? I looked at the other boaters, and smiled as the thought came, 'They can. So, damn me, can I.'

'Jimmy, look at her name.' A voice of disgust from Gay. I looked. There in large bold lettering was no 'Antigone' nor 'Dido' nor 'Electra'; nothing but the word 'Bawtry'. This I knew to be a place, but I had no idea where it was. The word was almost offensive, certainly unattractive. It was a sad blow, but there it must stay, for I would have no part in changing a ship's name.

The next few hours were spent in stowing our gear, making up the bed, and arranging somewhere around the cabins all the stores we had purchased. Then we went to the depôt store to collect the boats' gear and receive a shock. I had to make many journeys to and fro loaded with miles of different rope, from a cotton bow hauling tow-line to 'straps' to 'snatchers' and finally to a 'snubber'. Then back I went again for top cloths, fenders, shafts, cratch timber, dippers, cans and mops.

There was so much rope, so much of everything, that I remarked to the storeman, 'I'm only fitting out a pair, you know'. He smiled, leant across his counter and replied, 'You'll need all that's there, mate. And after your first trip you'll be in here begging for more. Like to take a bet?' I didn't.

By the end of the following week my hands were so stiff and my fingers so sore that it was painful to use them, but 'Bawtry' now looked like a proper working boat. The kind of tent which is called a 'cratch', an erection in the bows which, thanks be to God, remains erected, had quite defeated me. This and the correct manner of 'sheeting up', or covering the hold with heavy black tarpaulins, were the only tasks for which we asked help.

The depôt manager sent an elderly steerer along to do the explaining. This fellow examined my splices, back splices and effort on the cratch. He passed the rope work, but pulled the cratch to pieces, and put it all together again. He seemed to be very shy of us, and kept looking round to see if other steerers were watching. I had the feeling that he was ashamed to be helping us, and was hoping that his mates wouldn't catch him at it. Nevertheless he did a grand job, coiling and securing spare rope, and finishing everything off most neatly. For long in the future I was proud of the appearance of our butty, and, when our monkey boat was eventually ready, I altered her rope work to the same pattern.

* * * *

Life and activity in the lay-by interested us. Pairs came in. The P.A. system from the office cracked alive. Mumblings, mutterings, snatches of office conversation were heard, and then loud and clear a call: 'Will steerer Franks report to the office, please? Calling steerer Franks. Steerer Franks, please come to the office.' There followed a dreadful squealing noise and a loud click as the sound was cut.

Quite soon, chaffed by other steerers, a man walked along the hard, past the stern of our boat in the direction of the office. Later a diesel engine cracked into life. Her revolutions fell to a steady beat, and a pair nosed their way out of the lay-by, and headed down the cut towards Brentford's inland dock. Small, raggedly-clad children played along the concrete, yet not once did we see one fall into the water. Their older brothers and sisters went, screaming, to the depôt school. Women washed clothes in large galvanised-iron baths, and scrubbed out. Their men polished the brass loops and safety chains of the two range chimneys and engine exhaust stack; pipe-clayed the decorative cord-work on rudders, tillers and cratches, and cleaned the traditional paintwork of their boats—the roses and castles, diamonds and stars, and barber's pole painting on the tillers. Frequently they stopped for a yarn. Witticisms and jokes flew from boat to boat, while from within the cabins came the sounds of old battery radios.

We were left very much alone. There were no questions, no advice, just an occasional passing of the time of day. In fact, except that we caught the odd boater watching us from his cabin, in which case he immediately ducked, we might not have realized we were in any way unusual or of interest. We noticed particularly how they all averted their eyes when they passed our open cabin doors.

One afternoon the sudden frightening crackle of the P.A. line ripped the air. 'Calling steerer Fern. Steerer Fern come to the office, please.' I stood still. Other boaters looked around. 'Go on, stupid,' Gay called. 'That's you.' I knew this, but it came as a shock to hear my name through the system; also as a pleasure to be addressed as 'steerer' for the first time. Head high, I walked to the office, which was controlled by a friendly useful man called Mr Newbury—not 'John', 'George' or 'Jack' Newbury, but always 'Mr' Newbury.

'Your motor-boat is ready for you. You can collect it from the dry dock now.' He looked at me. All the head-high proud-of-being-called-steerer attitude drained suddenly from me. I was scared of making a dreadful mess of backing that 70-foot monster into the lay-by among all those boats, in front of the critical assemblage of professional steerers.

'God, I'm windy! Be a good fellow and have one of your captains take her down for me.'

'You've got to start sometime. Why not now?'

'Look, I'm prepared to start, but away from here, in the open. Just think of the damage I might do among all those boats.'

It had been a good remark. He considered the possibility. It must have frightened him as much as it did me, for he left the office and returned followed by a short, dark, youngish man with long sideboards, greased down, back-swept hair, a red choker and pointed yellow shoes.

'Steerer Hill will take her. Go with him and see how it's done. Mr Hill, meet Mr Fern. Put her alongside the butty with the extra cabin. O.K.?'

'O.K., Mr Newbury.'

We left the office. 'That your butty then?' he asked.

'Yes. You like her?'

'Cabin's orlright, but you've ruined the boat.'

'How?'

'Never get the load on. That's how. Nose heavy she'll be, or short on her loading. You'll see.'

I was annoyed, but excited to see our motor-boat. Damnation take them! Again no exotic or attractive name, but large on the cabin tumble home the word 'Chiswick'. So there we had them —'Chiswick' and 'Bawtry'—and it seemed difficult to think of two more horrible names.

The engine was ticking over. I cast off. Hill engaged reverse and opened the throttle. Very little happened except for a lot of noise. Hill thrust her into forward gear and roared the engine. She shivered and began to move ahead. He again put her in reverse and slammed the throttle open. Slowly she came to a halt, and began to pull backwards.

'Bleedin' prop's no bloody good!' he bawled. 'No draw. Bugger should be goin' like 'ell.'

We got her into position eventually, but Hill declared that she was 'right dangerous', and I, considering that reverse gear was the only form of braking for the two boats, felt a kind of panic at his remarks.

He left, and I began a check on the engine; then upped all the floorboards to check the shaft and its bearings. In the bilge were a great pile of mud, lumps of wood, a pair of shoes, a comb and the rusty mud-choked sieve of the bilge pump. I cleaned up this mess, started the engine, put her on a tick-over, engaged forward gear, and looked down again into the bilge. The shaft could not be said to be going round so much as up and down in a dignified loop, and the bearing caps, all loose, kept time with the rise and fall of the shaft. It was a fascinating but enraging sight, and the complete assembly was useless.

'Chiswick' went back to the engineers' sheds next day, and I was unpopular. However, no further attempts were made to pull my leg. She came back some days later after a trial run with the complete engineering staff, a few steerers, and two 10-hundredweight pigs of iron placed on the aft beam across the back end. Naturally, with all this weight aboard, she behaved more efficiently, and I accepted her but remained nervous about her performance astern.

There was little work for me to do on 'Chiswick', as she had not been freshly painted, which required stripping down all her gear. I improved her fenders, checked her side and top sheets, and spent most of my time in the engine-room. I cleaned and polished the engine, arranged tools, adjusted and tuned the dynamo and battery-charging gear, and generally made the place look ship-shape.

Gay hopped about from one boat to the other distributing our gear and stores, making lists of further requirements, dashing into Southall and returning with loaded shopping baskets. Except for her trousers, she already looked very much like other boating women of her age in her jerseys, her hair covered with a gay square, her feet in short leather sea-boots. Considering the activity of the life—the jumping, climbing in and out of steering cockpits, hurrying across lock gates, bicycling along towpaths—it was surprising that none of the younger women boaters wore trousers.

My gear was much the same as boatmen wore — just old clothes, with either heavy shoes or boots. Later, when we came to work our boats, I wore a cap to protect my eyes from the sun or driving rain. Apart from the fact that we looked shabby, there was nothing other than our windlasses—mine sticking out from my collar; Gay's hitched in her belt—to identify us as boaters.

By the end of the second week in December we were ready to start. I reported to Mr Newbury. He said, 'Good. I'll try to arrange an easy first trip for you. Your fuel and oil tanks are full, I suppose?'

'Good God, no!'

'Oh, I should see to that if I were you. You'll need fuel, you know.'

'All right, all right, I know. I'm a B.F. But isn't it wonderful how easily one can forget the most obvious?'

'It's been done before, I assure you. Fill her up, and if you leave the lay-by let me know when you'll be back. Soon now you can expect your first orders. Good luck, good boating, and come to me any time if you're in trouble. You've got our phone number. Just ring through. I'll know exactly where you are every day, so don't feel too lonely.'

We shook hands. I left the office thinking what a nice guy Mr Newbury was, and returned to the boats to tell Gay all about it. From then on, fuelling apart, we never left the lay-by. We just busied ourselves shaking down and studying my three-yards-long map of the Grand Union network, copied from one made by the famous Kit Gayford, the trainer of so many of the women who crewed these boats during the war. Kit's map was to prove invaluable to us. It showed not only all the locks and arms, but also the shops, pubs, water-taps; spots where milk, eggs and other things could be purchased; toll offices, telephones, tying-up places and, to Gay's delight, even where one might get a bath.

Every time the P.A. came to life, our hair stood on end. Not because we were nervous, but rather because we were longing to go. The feeling reminded me of sitting in an eight held at the stake-boat, waiting for the other crew to get straight, waiting for the umpire's, 'I'll ask you once, are you ready? Go!'

CHAPTER III

First Trip

'Calling steerer Fern. Steerer Fern to the office, please.'

'This is it. Put all that junk away, Gay. We're off.'

I leapt out of the butty, gained control of myself, walked slowly to the office and knocked.

'Come in. Oh hullo. Wish they were all as prompt as you. Orders. What's the time? 5.10 p.m. Well, no hurry. Leave tomorrow morning for Brentford, and load wood-pulp for Dickinson's Mill at Nash above Lock 68. Here are your orders. Have a good trip. I think you will. This is an easy one.'

'Right, and thanks. See you when we get back.'

I left the office, and ambled back to the pair, trying hard to look unconcerned. In the lay-by were a few steerers. They stared at me as I climbed aboard.

'What is it? Where's it to? Quick, tell me.' Gay seized the permit, and began to read. She looked up. 'Do we go now?'

'No. We'll have a good night's sleep, and be away at first light tomorrow.'

'Golly, it's exciting, isn't it? What do we get? Where's our rates book?'

'In the office section on the starboard shelf.'

She looked round the cabin, waved her right hand, her left, and turned to me. 'Oh stop fooling! Which is starboard anyway?'

'Your right. On the right, up for'ard there.'

She moved to the left.

'Your right, woman!'

'I never did know one from t'other. I'll learn one day.' She flicked the pages of the book.

'Oh goody! Seven bob a ton. How much shall we get on, do you think?'

'Fifty tons I hope, but we'll have to load it high aft.'

'That's your job. I'll do the accounts. Seven fives are thirty-five. Gracious! Three hundred and fifty shillings. It's money for jam.'

'We haven't got there yet. Wait until it's delivered. Then we'll think again. Come on to bed. We must be up bright and early. Alarm's set for six. How's that?'

'Oh, horrible! Do we really have to get up at six?'

'Three hundred and fifty shillings. Remember?'

'Oh yes. That's quite a lot of lolly. Up at six then. Move over a bit. I'm nearly in the hold.'

'Good night.'

'Good night.'

* * * *

'What's that damned noise?' I reached out and hit the top of the clock. Everything was black except the narrow, red, vertical lines between the bars of the small range. I dressed, made a pot of tea, took a cup to Gay and shook her. She complained as usual. I climbed from the cabin into the cold fresh air. Lights showed from other pairs, but everywhere was quiet. I crossed to the monkey boat, and lowered myself into the engine-room to make a final check.

Back in the butty Gay was cooking breakfast. I didn't even like the smell. We were quiet; neither wanted to talk. I reached for the calendar, flicked over one page, and under Friday, December 17, 1948, wrote, 'First orders. Off to Brentford.'

By about 8.30 a.m. everything was stowed away. We crept across to the monkey boat, trying to make as little noise as possible in order to avoid an audience, and wriggled down into the engine-room.

'Ready. You know what you've got to do?'

'O.K., boy. Swing her.' She giggled.

With both hands round the great starting handle, I began to turn the engine and flywheel—slowly at first, then faster, faster, faster. Then I called, 'Now'. Gay slammed down the first decompression tap, the engine fired, and all hell of a noise broke out. I slapped down the second tap, and away she went, evenly, on both cylinders. We left the room, closed the metal doors and cast off.

Our exit from the lay-by went well. Gay steered the butty, which was towed on a short snatcher. What a feeling to be away! Throttle open, good old engine throbbing ahead, water curling and gaily chasing along the bank, and astern the stem of the butty cutting my wake. Far behind was Gay, one arm leaning on the cabin, a hand on the long, down-curved, wooden tiller. I laughed. The blooming girl looked as if she had been steering seventy-feet boats all her life. In fact, until four months before, she had been acting in films and modelling expensive clothes.

As we approached Norwood top lock, I paled and swore. Ahead of us the whole canal was littered with barges and lighters. I cut the throttle and unhooked the snatcher from the hook on the counter. The butty moved up on me. I slung the snatcher on to her for'ard deck; then called loudly, 'Breast-up!' Gay, feeling saucy and no doubt pleased with herself, threw her chest out and pointed it at me.

'You're on your own, you know. If you don't get up for'ard quickly and fix your bow strap on to me, you'll go slap into that bunch.'

'Oh God, I forgot the front! Hey, hold this.' She tossed the stern strap, but it missed by yards, and away went the butty, passing quite swiftly, with Gay only half way along the catwalk to the bows. It was obvious that she would be far too late to couple at the bows, so I whipped open the throttle, and steered the motor-boat straight at the butty. She'd gone too far ahead. My bows hit her aft of midships. She curled away across my bows, and continued on her course smack into the right bank, taking a surprised Gay with her deep into the bushes. The motor-boat continued ahead. Not only had I forgotten to engage neutral, or better still reverse, but, fascinated at the antics of the butty and her crew, I had steered towards the left bank which was now close. It was no good. Everything went wrong. The gear wheel stuck in 'ahead' position. The boat's answer to the tiller was far too slow. We drove hard into the mud.

'Not exactly professional, and very unkind of you,' Gay bawled from the far bank.

'It's all your silly fault. You should know better than to fool about like that. We must have some discipline on these boats. When I say "breast-up", get up for'ard smartish.'

There we stood, one on either bank—our boats crossed, their

bows munched into the mud on opposite sides—and just roared with laughter.

It took a bit of pushing and heaving on the long pole before we regained order, but soon the boats were neatly breasted, and I walked down the towpath to find out the reason for the hold-up. In the top lock was a lighter, and five others were waiting to go down the flight of eight locks.

I looked at my watch. 9.15. I looked again when we were through. It was 1.45!

On we went, still breasted, boats alongside one another, cross-strapped at bow and stern. Gay's tiller on the cabin trunk resting with its end between her elbows. We rounded the last bend, and there ahead the cut opened out into the wide expanse of Brentford Dock. Now we are in the dock, passing close to pairs moored along the right bank. I note where the line of empty boats finishes on the opposite bank, for there we must make fast. I am seized by a great longing to do what Herbert Chitty told us was the neatest, most difficult piece of steering—to turn a breasted pair in one great sweep in Brentford Basin.

I look at the gap and think. The throttle is wide open. We seem to be tearing past boats, and as we go boater's heads pop from hatches. As they peek at us, up go their hands to their hats. Women peer above their gun'ales, turn pale, grab their young and duck. The men, all smiles, toss words of warning and lean on cabin-tops to watch the fun.

Smiles or leers? Damn me, I've got a critical audience. I'm inspired. I make up my mind, and call loudly to Gay, 'Stand by. We're turning in one.'

'You can't. You'll never do it. You'll bust them all up and us too. Only boaters can wind a pair in one. Don't be daft, Jimmy.'

'Too late. We're off.'

'Oh my God, I'm going. I can't stand it!'

She darts down into her cabin, and I'm alone. Just as well perhaps. I take one more look. The position's right; speed right. Nobody else moving. It's all ours. Now—and over goes the tiller, hard over. I check the throttle—it's wide open. I work the tiller against the angry, boiling, white lump of water swirling from under the counter. The pair begin to turn. Their speed slackens. They shiver. But those distant stems move slowly round. Now we are headed for the boats moored on the far side of the dock.

From them steerers leap ashore. I smile and think, 'Because, if anything goes wrong, their boats will sink.'

I sweep with the tiller, feel very hot, talk to the boats. 'Come round, come round, my beauties.'

As the gap closes, my nerve nearly fails. There, ahead, five or six steerers, shoulder to shoulder, silently watching. They're gone now from my sight, which is focused on the incessantly changing scene beyond the turning stems. It's too late to stop them now. 'Come on. You've got to go round.' Again I check the throttle; work the tiller. They answer. We are almost round, rushing past moored boats, the gap closing swiftly. At last, up for'ard, there, only water. I cut the throttle right back, slam her into reverse and feel her shivering in complaint. I hear the deep growling sound of infuriated water eddying under the hulls, and notice that the space between us and the last moored pair is only inches. We ease into the bank. I bellow to Gay, 'For'ard mooring line. We've made it!'

She shoots from her cabin and looks around to be satisfied that we really have winded. Then she tears along the top planks and stands on the fore deck, rope in hand, ready to make the jump ashore.

There's no need. Steerers are already there to take her line. Two come aft for mine. One says, 'Good work, Captain,' and they make us fast. Again I looked at my watch. It was 2.30 p.m., and we had been six hours travelling five miles.

As soon as the steerers had gone, Gay and I had a blazing row. She said my feat of winding had been plain silly. I knew there was a deal of truth in this, but I wasn't going to admit it.

'If you go on playing daft tricks like this, we'll be wrecked almost before we have started. Besides you scared the lights out of me, and all the other steerers too.'

Perhaps she was right about this also, but, looking back, we know that our relationships with the boaters changed from that day onwards. Maybe they realized that we meant to work, and had not just come to play. Until this event we had been made to feel different, that we did not belong. Henceforward, and as trip followed trip, we received every kind of assistance from them, and came to like them more and more. Eventually we were trusted by them, accepted. In fact before very long they were coming to us with various and extraordinary requests.

We reported our arrival to the man in charge of the Dock Office, who told us that loading our pair would not start until 8 a.m. the following day. We were free to do as we pleased. We had a meal; then strolled into the town. London is a city of many villages, and Brentford is one—at least down the end by the cut. Here are small steamed-up cafés, the menus chalked on the windows above lace curtains. An ironmonger's shop is truly a village store, and inside one must move cautiously for fear of tumbling the fantastic stock. There are old pubs, and old buildings, mostly small; a fish-and-chip shop, and suddenly a window filled with handsome decorated pottery. We entered the shop behind the showroom, and met a charming, elderly, Austrian Jew, who was working at his wheel. In another room was his kiln.

'No, much zorrow, but I haf none of these vases. Ja, ja, I know how you mean. Not to stant, but 'ang from the valls. Ja, ja, vall-vase. I am zo zorry. I haf none, but I vill make them just for you. No, pleece. You zay. I make.'

Outside I asked Gay, 'What do you want them for?'

'Our cabins, of course. We must have some flowers.'

'But these are working boats, not yachts.'

'Never mind. We may come to look scruffy. Our boats may not be beautiful. But inside they will always be clean, and must look like home.'

We walked on, past a small draper's shop and an even smaller butcher's, where a vast man stood behind a bloody block, shining chopper held in bloody hand, sporting a bloodstained blue-and-white apron and immaculate straw boater. We went on up the village street until, quite suddenly, it changed; became more modern. Two or three of the original frontages had been knocked into one large showroom, with chromium plate. Double-decker buses swung across the road and away up to Ealing. There was a great dark building on the right, foreign and stinking of gas. We retraced our steps after crossing the road, and before long heard a voice calling, 'Pleece, meester, pleece'.

We saw our Austrian friend beckoning from his door, and crossed over. 'Com, com mit me.' We re-entered his shop. He hurried to the back room, and returned bearing a wet wall-vase, not yet clean. He placed it in Gay's hands, and said, 'Of a sudden

I remember my paint brushes. You zee I haf zem on ze vall. It is for you.'

'Oh but . . . ' began Gay.

'No, no. Pleece, for you.' He offered the vase to Gay.

'But I must pay you . . . '

'It is nutting. I like you to haf it.' Determined, he folded his hands behind him. 'You take it, goot. That makes me 'appy.'

We accepted the vase. It endured countless disasters on the boats, and hangs here, now, reminding us always of one charming Jew who escaped in time.

Our holds were cleared by 8 the following morning, but it was not until 11.20 that loading of the butty started. At five that evening the pair were still not loaded. On Sunday the men continued with the job, and by 9 a.m. our consignment of 298 bales was aboard. With a hoist capable of lifting only two bales at a time, loading took five hours.

We began sheeting up as best we could. In no time three steerers arrived to help, one of them being Hill, who had warned me about the monkey boat's poor performance in reverse gear. This task completed, we let go, breasted and backed slowly towards Lock 100, the toll lock where the boats were gauged to discover the weight of our cargo. We were given a Permit Sheet, Trip Card, and Delivery Note in duplicate.

By 10.45 a.m. we were ready to start our first trip. Quietly, so that the Toll Officer should not hear, Gay whispered, 'It says 50 tons. Now to deliver it, and collect our lolly. I'm all set. Are you?'

'Yep. On our way.'

I opened the throttle gently, went ahead up the length of the butty, leant across and took the snubber from 'Bawtry's' cratch. I flicked it round a stud and on to the hook on 'Chiswick's' counter, and watched it pay out, then tauten and begin its ceaseless complaints under strain. The butty heeled a little and began to follow. I opened the throttle wider. A ripple grew round 'Bawtry's' cut-water, and we were away.

* * * *

Gay said it was all my fault, and I suppose she was right. I had forgotten that the Norwood Flight was locked on Sundays at noon. We arrived there at exactly 12.07, and found the chains already on. This meant mooring and waiting until 6 on Monday morning.

We swore, railed against officials, who did not wish to work as hard as we, washed down our paintwork, went for a walk, and turned in early.

At 4 next morning we were about in a cold dark world. Before 6 the engine was started. By 7.40 we were through the locks and away along the seven-miles stretch to Cowley; then through Uxbridge. We were doing fine when, rounding a bend, we found the road blocked by two lighters piled high with timber and creeping along in tow behind a small motor-boat. We trailed them, for I hadn't the nerve to overtake that lot.

Eventually, after what seemed like hours of crawling, this gaggle pulled into a wharf. As we passed, I gave vent for the first time to my feelings as a frustrated boater, and bellowed, 'Why didn't you pull over and let us pass? Do you want the whole bloody cut for yourself and your blasted wood?'

The skipper of the tug told me to take a running jump and stuff myself up my chimney. By now, free and laughing, I had passed, and was quite surprised to hear my mate aft piping up in dreadful language, shouting about 'bloody old barges which shouldn't be allowed to get in the way, and vulgar tug-men who are rude to their betters'.

Perhaps this temper-losing was frowned upon by the gods, because shortly afterwards the engine revolutions suddenly fell, and black smoke blew upwards from the exhaust stack. 'Ah, I know all about this one,' I thought. 'Something in the propeller.' I banged her into reverse and blipped the throttle; then let it out and went ahead again. No good, no revs., just smoke. We crawled ahead towards Lock 86, and there, boat-hook in hand, I went ashore and began hooking away at the propeller. There was something there right enough, something hard, metallic. I heaved and won about a yard, but could pull no further. I called to Gay to get aboard the monkey boat.

'Don't move the throttle. Just ease in the gear; then whip it out. Just a touch mind.' Meanwhile I hauled on the hook. Well, she did her best no doubt, but few women seem to have any feeling, any sense of touch, where machinery is concerned. She smartly and firmly screwed the damned thing into full ahead, and took a long time to unscrew it back to neutral. This I surmised only, for I was far too busy to watch. What happened at my end was that quite suddenly, instead of standing on the bank, I was hitched swiftly into the cut, and beaten about by a flaying pole ten feet long. In fact the slack won was suddenly taken up again, and whatever it was around the prop now entwined the hook also.

Nervously, after some heated explanation, we tried reversing the engine. I retrieved the hook and again a yard, but no more. Things looked bad to us both, but, thanks be, I could hear a pair coming along fast and soon, round a bend they came, apparently without a steerer. We were both alarmed and amazed. The boat, headed straight for us, was going flat out, without anyone at the helm.

'Wonderful. Just look at that.' Gay pointed.

'I am looking. If someone doesn't take over soon, the whole outfit will crash into us.'

'No. Look behind the cabin.'

I looked, and saw a small head. The pair were controlled by a young boy not yet tall enough to show above the height of the cabin. In a moment a man appeared, took over, executed a perfect breasting-up, and brought his pair alongside the bank aft of us. Hill, of course! We had a chat. His wife and son who, he told us, was nine years of age and a good steerer, took over his boats and worked them through the lock, while he showed us how to clear the prop. Even for such an experienced man as this it was hard going, and it took us three-quarters-of-an-hour, by the end of which we had thirteen feet of barbed wire lying on the towpath.

We thanked him for both his assistance and teaching. He made little of it, only remarking that there were tricks to learn. We were not to worry. In fact we were doing well.

Free once again, delighted by Hill's remark, and eager to be on our way, we worked harder and faster. We passed through Lock 86, through 85. Now, of course, Hill having gone ahead, all the locks were against us. Then, with 84 a few lengths only away, I put the motor-boat hard aground while cutting a corner.

It was 5 p.m. when we arrived at Rickmansworth, which is a permitted place for mooring at night. We had neither eaten nor had a drink for thirteen hours. We decided to call it a day, and made fast below the lock with the butty inside. Now, with engine cut and everything quiet, we suddenly felt exhausted, and realized that we ached everywhere. Norwood seemed days back. We lowered ourselves down the steps into the warm cabin of the butty, switched on the light and the portable radio, and took our boots off. The great kettle was singing away, Gay made a strong pot of tea. I reached into a cupboard and withdrew a bottle of rum, purchased and stowed for medicinal purposes only. 'How do you feel, Gay?'

'Terrible. A case of nervous exhaustion. And you?'

'Bad, very bad. A case of shock.'

We used tumblers, one-third rum, two-thirds dark hot sweet tea. Wonderful medicine.

* * * *

We rose at 5.30 next morning, cast off at 7.40 and eased into Lock 81. All went well for a while, and I was just beginning to enjoy my boating when, for no obvious reason, the monkey boat quite suddenly went aground. Details of everything which took place would be a bore. It took us two-and-a-half hours to travel one mile. Without the help of a lock-keeper and some lengthmen, we should never have got that far.

I took soundings right across the cut at Croxley, and nowhere was there more than three feet of water. The watermark along the banks was twelve and fourteen inches above the actual water level, and all who helped agreed that the monkey boat had been loaded nose heavy; was in fact down by the bows.

To get us moving, somebody opened the paddles of Lock 78. Down came water, and immediately we were away. It sounds a simple enough remedy, but, by borrowing water from a higher pound, one frequently brings further trouble when that pound is reached, and this is precisely what happened. Away from 78 we went, flat out, but in no time our speed slackened, and we began to churn along. Up behind the counter came mud, leaves, twigs and stink. Throttle wide open, we crept forwards.

A pair of Harvey Taylor's boats loaded with sand approached. The motor-boat was almost past me when it went aground. Up came the butty, struck it, bounced off and hit me a crack. Over went my bows, firmly into mud. We tried everything — full astern, full ahead, shoving with long poles—and all was useless.

The steerer's wife let fly a sizzling strip of coarse oaths, cursing the cut, the mud, the lack of water. An elegant uniformed park-keeper ambled along the towpath, stood gazing at us and laughed. I wanted to get at him, to do something, but there we all were, stuck on the middle of the cut, unable to reach the banks.

After a while we heard the music of rising and falling pawls. Someone was letting down water from 77. In time the other pair pulled away, leaving me heaving, prodding, poking with a long shaft until my shoulders and stomach were bruised and my hands nearly paralyzed.

We got off eventually, and crept towards the lock, but again stuck fast at its entrance. Three lengthmen helped us out of this fix. Forward went the monkey boat, but when she was two-thirds of the way into the lock she halted. Her stem was fouling the sill.

I was feeling weak from lack of food, exhausted and dispirited, and now came this disaster from which I could see no way out. This was a mechanical problem, not one of brute force. How can one lift 25 tons of cargo and 15 tons of boat up over a concrete step? It is obviously impossible, one might think, but there is a way, and it was shown to us by a man who suddenly appeared on a bicycle. He was tall, and wore an old cap, with a stained raincoat. He had a warm smile, a quiet voice.

'Cast off your butty. Back the monkey half-way down the length of the lock. Hold her there against the inrush of water when I lift the paddles. I'll then drop them and yell. You, open the throttle. She'll come ahead over the sill. Smack her into reverse quickly to lessen the blow when your for'ard fender strikes the lock. Got it?'

'Yes, but I don't follow how . . . '

'You will. Now get down there and watch me.'

I did as he said, but still could not see how he reckoned to lift the boat over the sill. She was in gear now. He wound up the paddles on the top gates. A great mass of water poured down into the lock, surged around the boat, passed beneath it and charged out of the open lower gates. 'Chiswick' tried to go astern with the rushing water, I held her against it on the throttle. She careered round and struck the walls, but I kept her in position. This sudden and massive influx of water set up a wave outside the lock gates. The wave rolled away down the pound. As quickly as our friend had opened the paddles he now dropped them. The noise of crashing water ceased. I eased the throttle back to a tick over, and looked aft.

'Keep your eyes on me.'

Quickly I turned and watched him. My heart suddenly seemed to miss a beat or two with sheer excitement, for I had seen something and now understood. The wave which had charged down into the pound was now rolling back towards the lock. I fingered the throttle and checked the gear lever, never taking my eyes from the smiling face above. He was watching aft, standing still, and then up went his hands, 'Now. Give it to her. Come on. Come ahead!'

Ye gods, I did too. But what a mess I made of winding her from ahead to astern. We went in, right in, with a hell of a crash, and the blow we struck the top gates knocked me off my feet down the steps into the cabin.

'Where you gone to, Captain?'

Our friend was laughing now. What a man! He stayed with us, helping all the time. On we went slowly but surely. We worked through from 77 to 69, when again we stuck hard at the entrance. But another pair had come up astern, and the steerer, who might have passed us and taken the lock, instead slowed down, brought his bows up to my stern and together we just shoved her in.

So to 68, the last lock. Through this we passed, and, with just a quarter of a mile to go, we were again creeping along and churning up the bottom, when slowly we came to a standstill right alongside a moored pair. A woman looked out of the butty and called, 'Aye. We stook there yesterday, and couldna move neither.' Then she retreated into the warmth and brightness of her home. We were in darkness, and a pair were coming up fast astern. I wondered if they could do any better. Evidently the crew thought so, because they came on flat out, missing us by inches. But it wasn't to happen. Neatly, as they were alongside, boat by boat, they came to a halt. Now there were six of us.

Too exhausted to do anything, I just stood and waited, not knowing or even thinking what I was waiting for. But I couldn't have done better. Through the darkness came a voice, one we knew, one we were happy to hear, the voice of Mr Hill. The amazing Mr Hill—first at the depôt, then unwinding wire in Widewater, and now at Nash. What a man! What a saviour!

Again rose the sweet sound of rattling pawls. Down came water, and ahead we crept until Mr Hill could take our headline and wind us round into the short Nash Mill cut.

We had arrived—bruised, bleeding, bewildered, starved and in a stupor. Eleven lumps of flesh were missing from my hands, and a large lump from a leg as a result of the sudden smart descent into the cabin. My trousers in front were soaked from handling the cold dripping snubber, and at the back from sitting on wet banks pushing with my feet.

It was 5.15 p.m. We had been on the move for 9 hours 35 minutes, travelling 8 miles 2 furlongs. It was 11 hours 45 minutes since our day had started, and again we had gone without food or drink.

Down in the butty's bright warm cabin Gay asked, 'How do you feel, Jimmy?'

'Oh fine. On top of the world. We've done it anyway.'

'What a wonderful man Mr Hill is. And that smiling man, who was he? Where did he get to?'

'I wonder. Didn't even see him go. Fortunately I thanked him —and from the bottom of my heart. How do you feel?'

'Me?' She smiled. 'I'm buggered.'

* * * *

To say we slept well that night would be an under-statement. What we really did was to pass out for thirteen hours. When we regained consciousness, it was bright daylight, and Hill's pair were still being unloaded.

We spent the next eight hours cleaning our boats and ropes, eating, talking to Hill and holding our own conference upon the troubles and disasters of the first trip.

Hill, as usual, was helpful. 'I told you back in the depôt you'd be in trouble.'

'How? What do you mean?'

'That there cabin. To get 50 tons aboard they've overloaded the monkey. For future, on bulky cargoes, you want slack boards on your butty aft, and load high in the back end.'

'Slack boards?'

'Yer, like raisin' the gun'ales. Timber, boards, one atop the other on a frame, holes in the top boards so you can rope 'em across and make all safe.'

'I follow. That certainly is an idea.'

'Yer. Now come here, mate.' He took me to the bow of his monkey boat. 'See these lines. Well, never load her so *that* line is under water. Up to there's O.K., and, if I was you, I'd always load me motor first, and anything what's left over must go aboard the butty. She mustn't go below'—we moved to the bows of his butty—'here, see. If you're loaded down to where I showed you, you're full, and better refuse any more.'

'It took us twenty-two hours to get here from Brentford. How long were you on the journey?'

'We came through non-stop, darkness and all. Took us eighteen hours.'

'Eighteen! You were only four hours faster than we were?'

'Can't go so quick in the dark, in spite of lights. Besides, we had our troubles too. Level's down, and the cut wants dredgin'. All they do is muck about with a bloody big spoon. Dredgin'! These days they orter have a machine. Spoonin' it out is useless, just bloody useless!'

I was in complete agreement with him, and, in view of all our worries, his next remark amused me.

'You can't have your chimneys like that. You must get some brass on 'em—three brass bands spaced even like, and a nice brass chain to secure 'em. Yours is not proper. Don't look right.'

Gay and I discussed our experiences and agreed on various points: (1) we must eat during the day; (2) most of our troubles would have been either less serious or perhaps non-existent if we had not been incorrectly loaded; (3) we must go more slowly under bridges and into locks; (4) we must try not to be in such a hurry generally. Then our boating might become more of a pleasure. For instance, here we sat waiting to be unloaded.

Indeed, it was not until 4.30 that we drew the butty into position near the crane. They worked on her for an hour, and then went away for the day. At 8.45 next morning unloading began again, and at 3.30 we were away heading for Lock 68.

Our progress interested me, particularly our performance in reverse, because, somewhat against my better feelings, I had taken Hill's advice and poured hundreds of buckets full of water into the bilges beneath the motor-boat's counter. But of course he was right. The performance astern was vastly improved, which meant that with this, so to speak, increased braking power we could risk going faster.

What a difference from two days back! Now we really enjoyed our boating. I had the butty up close aft on crossed straps, Gay steering. Had I been cleverer at the game, she need not have steered, because, when one knows how, it is possible for the monkey-boat steerer also to control the butty when it is thus hitched. The system works rather as does an articulated motor vehicle. If the stern of the powered boat passes through a gap, the bows of the one on tow must also, as they are so tightly secured one to another; but the stern of the towed boat is seventy feet aft and may be out of alignment. If one wishes to move this stern to the right, one moves the stern of the powered boat to the left, which takes the bows of the towed boat to the left and moves its stern to the right, and of course *vice versa*. This all sounds complicated, but is, with sufficient practice, very simple, as any experienced articulated-vehicle driver would assert. But try steering one of these vehicles for the first time, say through an archway and into a certain position in a yard, and you will then understand why Gay steered.

We cracked along the pounds admiring the scenery. Every now and then I cut back the throttle in order to yell something at the mate and have some chance of her hearing. We worked the locks in a splendid manner, each to an allotted task. We began to think we were pretty experienced and efficient boaters.

Darkness came quickly, and, although we were in open country and had promised ourselves a beer this night, we moored, considering it wiser to play the game safely in our early days rather than push on towards Watford and possibly pile up on some unexpected bend.

We were up at 5.30 next morning—Christmas Eve—and had washed, cooked breakfast, cleaned up and were on the move by 7.15. During the next nine hours we travelled eighteen miles through nineteen locks, seventeen of which were against us. Two miles an hour on a bad road such as this was good going for beginners. We made fast in the lay-by at the depôt by 4.30 p.m. and were feeling proud of ourselves and somewhat surprised to be back in one piece at the place we had actually left eight days previously (which anyway seemed nonsense; it must surely have been at least a month). We were also excited to have arrived in time to spend Christmas at Richmond with the family.

We turned off all the taps and switches; clipped padlocks on the engine-room and cabin doors, and walked along to report our arrival and departure to Mr Newbury in the office. 'Boaters!' He laughed. 'One trip and you're back on the land as fast as possible. Well done. Have a merry Christmas. Let me know when you're back. I'll find you a tougher one for your next trip.'

'Good,' said Gay, 'but make sure it's at a fat rate. We'll be broke by then.'

'Tougher!' I thought. 'I hope we never have to face anything tougher than our first.'

At home I completed the log. The final figures were interesting:

Round trip of	8 days
Total distance	52 miles
Time on move	35 hours 39 minutes
Time loading	5 hours 5 minutes
Time unloading	5 hours 10 minutes
Fuel oil consumed	23 gallons
Lubricating oil consumed	1 gallon
Rate (net)	7 shillings
Tonnage	50 tons
Into kitty	£17 10 0
Remarks	Bloody but unbowed

CHAPTER IV

Steel for Birmingham

We returned to our boats a few days after Christmas, and on the same afternoon received orders to report to the Shipping Clerk in Regent's Canal Dock for loading with steel billets to be delivered at Tyseley Wharf, Birmingham.

Soon after 4 p.m. we left the lay-by, and a little over three hours later moored at Hampstead Road top lock, fifteen miles away. Between were no locks. With empty boats and the cut deserted, as most of the journey was in darkness, we averaged nearly five miles an hour. It was an exciting, fascinating journey past lighted railway depôts, great gas works and large blocks of offices in which lights cut off as workers left for their homes. We went under Ladbroke Grove, past the slums of Westbourne Green to Maida Hill, through the tunnel with an ear-splitting roar and out the other side with weeping eyes into Regent's Park. And there ahead were the locks.

We made fast alongside a pitted, worn towpath liberally studded with horse-droppings. Down by the cut it was pitch dark still, and the air smelled more of horses than diesel. Dim lights shone from the cabin portholes of other moored pairs. A diving rat plopped into the water. A sash-cord ran over a squealing pulley. A door banged. These sounds alone broke the quiet. We stood listening, and looking upon a scene unchanged for a hundred years. Then, suddenly, a double-decker bus shot across a distant bridge and headed in the direction of the West End.

'Let's dress up and go into London.' Gay looked excited. The idea amused me. We washed, changed from our canal clothes and in a few minutes were on a bus. Much later, tongues loosened by all the beers we had drunk in our old haunts round Piccadilly, Soho and Shepherd's Market, we stepped down on to the towpath away from the lights and noise of the streets above.

'You know what fascinates me so much about this life?'

'No, what?' Gay asked.

'It seems to me that we are living in two eras.'

'How do you mean?'

'The great canal epoch and the modern age. Whenever I dress up and we step away from the cut, I feel the same. We leave the past and return to our own times.'

'Ah, but we have an engine. That makes us modern.'

'Not for me. It's almost the only false note. Think of the women—dark-skinned, black plaited hair wound round their heads, boots, long skirts. The towpaths in these parts—horse manure everywhere and the deep imprints of hooves.'

'I know. I just trod right into one, and I'm wearing a lovely pair of open-toed shoes.'

'Oh, don't bring us back so sharply to practical matters. I was remembering Berkhamsted thirty years ago. It was nearly all horses then. It's fascinating to be at last on the cut.'

'Look, you can stand here and dream if you like, but I'm getting cold. I'm going down.'

She stepped aboard, undid the padlock on the door and switched on the lights in the cabin. They pierced the darkness suddenly; insulted the scene. She drew the doors together. The garish light vanished. Only beams from the curtained portholes cut the gloom, and all was right again.

That child's dreams of leaving his straitened world were taking shape. We had been up the cut some distance. We were in the great city with our boats. Tomorrow we would pass right across London, down to Limehouse, and into the dock by the Thames. The dreams were fast becoming realities, but I felt sure that the reality would be vastly different from the dream.

We were away down the locks at first light, and in less than an hour arrived at the entrance to Islington Tunnel. Ahead was an empty breasted pair, the steerer waving us down and into the side.

'What's wrong?' I bellowed.

'Same as usual. Bloody barge stook in tunnel.'

'This often happen then?'

'Too often, mate. Silly buggers will overload them. Like as not it's timber or fibre bales.'

For two hours and fifty minutes we sat on our bottoms waiting. Then a small tug emerged towing a huge timber-loaded barge, which was followed by three pairs of narrow boats. As each pair overtook the barge, a slanging match ensued. Women and children as well as the men loosed streams of oaths at one another; then, when almost out of hearing, ended by saying, 'Goodbye then', or 'Cheerio, duckie', and waving fond farewells.

On through Hoxton to Shoreditch, past the junction with the Hertford Union Canal, under the Mile End Road, through Stepney. We passed through mile after mile of endless slums, with acres of cleared ground, mountains of rubble, heaps of charred timbers, the ghoulish evidence and refuse of bombing. We passed great soaring blocks of human hutches, square monstrosities in brick entwined by iron stairways, with windows cluttered by china Alsatians and plastic flowers. Finally and thankfully we entered one of the twin Commercial Road locks, and came out under a railway bridge and into the crowded expanse of Regent's Canal Dock. On the left was a long jetty, its end free of craft. I put my tiller over, made a great sweep and brought the pair alongside.

We reported our arrival, and were told that the ship from which we should be loaded had not yet berthed, and it would probably be some time on Monday morning when we should be wanted. It was Saturday afternoon. I asked, 'Can we leave the boats and get out of here for a walk?' The phone on the man's table rang. 'Hang on a minute,' he said. We hung on and on. That conversation lasted for about fifteen minutes. At the end of it he looked up and said, 'She'll be in tomorrow evening. You load early. Do what you like, but be ready first thing Monday. Holds clear, chains unfastened. O.K.?'

'O.K. and thanks.' We left the office.

On Sunday evening we were sitting, one either side of the upturned butty tiller, on the gun'ales, smoking, listening to the distant sounds of ships' sirens and catching a glimpse through the darkness of coloured lights, as vessels passed the far end of the great lock opposite us on their way up, or down, the river. The dock was quiet; lighters, barges and narrow boats still. Three merchantmen, their portholes aglow, rode alongside the quays. Someone, smoking a cigarette, stood on the swingbridge which carried Narrow Street across the lock. In the nearby keeper's office many lights were burning.

Suddenly the whole scene changed. On went brilliant flood-lights. Bellowed orders echoed round the dock. Men hurried from lighted buildings, and bustle expelled serenity.

The swing-bridge was folded away; the Thames-side lock gates opened. Beyond, high up, we saw port and starboard lights, with, much higher, a mast-head light. Our ship had arrived.

Sedately, little by little, to the sounds of bells and commanding voices, she eased into the lock. Her for'ard deck was illuminated. Hawsers were passed overside, and she was made fast. In due time the inner gates were opened, the ship freed and slowly, very slowly, she came ahead, right towards us.

We stood, a few inches only above water-level, watching the high stem advancing upon us and hoping like hell they would swing her before this bow of steel cleft our hulls. We raised our eyes, and there, way above, shone the mast-head light. There was no sign of any look-out, and still she crept ahead. At last, with her stern clear of the lock, the for'ard warps tightened and the stem veered. She was winched around and berthed along the South Quay.

The lock gates crunched together. The bridge reappeared. Lights were extinguished, and it became quiet again in the dock. We heaved sighs of relief, and went below.

At 11 on the Monday morning we were ordered alongside the ship, and loading started. Great lengths of steel billets soared from the ship, swung crazily through the air above the heads of the two loaders in our hold, and came sizzling down on top of them. To me it was a dreadful sight; to them—nothing. A few feet above their heads the load stopped and spun. Then, when it was at last in line, down it came into the loaders' reach. They shoved it into position. Then came the final drop. The boat heeled over, and a crashing and falling noise came from the cabin.

Out shot Gay's head. 'Tell those blighters to be more gentle. The crocks are flying everywhere.'

'You tell 'em, but I don't think they'll take much notice.' Gay leant backwards, looked up towards the cabin of the crane, shook her small fist and screamed, 'Take it easy, you silly oaf. You're wrecking my home.' He up there waved to her with one hand, and dumped the second load with the other. Up came the butty to an even keel, and Gay nearly shot out over the side into the dock. This was enough for her. She retreated into the comparative safety of the cabin.

The loading intrigued me. The brave fellows in our hold rarely seemed to give any signals. They talked all the time, and leapt away from the thrashing chains as they were ripped upwards from under the billets. The whole business seemed dangerous and far too hurried, and it resulted in considerable damage to the woodwork of the boats.

I kept a careful watch on our load lines to make certain that the mistake of our first trip was not repeated, and, as soon as we neared the marks, I refused any more billets, and pulled the pair away from the ship to a quiet spot where we could sheet up. By 4 we were clear of the dock, and had begun the climb up to Paddington Bar. We worked until 6 that evening, and made fast below Old Ford Lock.

Keen to be on our way and make a quick trip, we were up early on the Tuesday, and, working in darkness, reached the entrance to Islington Tunnel just before 8 a.m. Here we found five pairs and eleven barges blocking the cut. Again a lighter, this time loaded with bales of fibre, was stuck in the tunnel. We made fast and waited.

After failing to force this overloaded craft through to the far end, they pushed it backwards, and it was disgorged into the array of twenty-one assorted vessels. The shambles that followed was impressive. Hull crashed against hull. Narrow boats were pounded and ground into the banks, their wooden cabins cracking, being torn and deeply scratched. Above all this noise rose the din of dozens of persons shouting instructions, and cursing.

Our boats were damaged. The surface of the butty cabin was torn. They were squeezed out of shape, and used by bargees with long-shafted hooks either to hang on to or push from. These bargees reckoned the whole scene was pretty good fun. They marched about their hulking vessels laughing, joking and slinging cracks across the canal. In the water, bales of fibre bobbed around, and the surface was matted with fibre torn from broken bales.

After this infernal experience we made good headway under pleasant but cold conditions. Beyond Hampstead Road locks the cut was level to Cowley, about twenty miles away, and there, at 5.30 in the evening we tied up below the lock, wondering just how far we might have gone had we not been held up for over two hours at Islington.

The only other annoying event took place on the really devilish turn at the junction of the R.C. Dock arm with the main arm at Bull's Bridge. It was almost opposite the lay-by and in full view of all the depôt folk. I took the bend too quickly, and Gay, though sweeping hard with her great tiller, was unable to bring the butty right round fast enough. She struck the bank a glancing blow only, but it was sufficient to keel the boat over to a terrifying angle. I had cut the throttle and was busy heaving in the great long snubber when she arrived alongside. 'Hey, don't you play that game. It may be easier for you to turn at speed, but just try getting this beast round.'

'Sorry. My fault. Are you all set now?'

'Yes, I'm recovering . . . Well go on. Don't let's hang around here. We're supposed to be going to Brum.'

* * * *

Our lives now began to settle down. Each day was much like another in some respects, but in others very different. We rose every morning at about 4.30, and worked until dark. Around noon we had a short rest, a drink and a bite of something cold. When the going was not too difficult, Gay produced a cup of tea during the afternoon. That wonderful kettle sat on top of the range just inside and on the left of the butty cabin. By holding the end of her long tiller, or letting it go for a minute along a straight stretch, she could dart down into the cabin, make the tea and pop up again before anything untoward happened. Or in a lock I would work all the paddles and gates while she produced the food.

We worked hard at improving our boating, most particularly our breasting-up before closed locks, and our entries into those open and ready to receive us. We came to appreciate the significance of the finger signs given by lock-wheelers or crews of pairs passing in the opposite direction. Up would go one, three, maybe even five fingers. Cheery greetings were given and received, and then we understood that one, three or five locks were ready for us, a 'good road' ahead. In these early days we were frequently overtaken, and, being newcomers — 'trainees' as the boaters called us—we did our best to help, and nothing to annoy or slow them down.

The weather was all-important. When it was dry or sunny we went along much faster than when it rained. Then we had to wear oilskins, which hampered jumping around, and generally got in the way. Rain also made things slippery, and more care had to be taken on wet lock-gates. Strong winds, especially on the beam, were the devil. With empty boats one went sideways along the pounds, with bows bearing up all the time into the wind. Often, when we were coming slowly ahead out of locks, it took hold of our bows and swept them across into the leeward bank. With loaded boats it was not as bad, but in times of full gale, when we were sheeted up, we would be blown right off course if we were not careful.

Every day brought its excitements and shocks. We came quickly to appreciate how cautious one must be until one knew the road. However, it was fun and rewarding to be on the move all day through a ceaselessly changing pattern of countryside, even though our progress, as yet, was slow.

From Cowley we worked our way steadily along the course of our first trip, and were delighted to find how much easier it was when we were not overloaded and knew exactly what snags to expect around the next bend. Soon we were past Nash and the never-to-be-forgotten Lock 68; past Fishery Inn at Boxmoor. We came to Berkhamsted, which is just a matter of one lock after another, each officially numbered and well named by generations of boaters—Winkwell, Sewerage, Broadwater, Gas Two, Bushes and finally—Cowroast. This is Lock 46, the end of the great climb up from London and along the edge of the Chiltern Hills—a matter of fifty-seven locks in fifty-five miles.

Cowroast meant much to us. It was more than a summit. If we were going up country we stopped here a while for a breather. The worst section was over. From here it was downhill for a while, into more open country with many fewer locks. If we were coming back to London we stopped for a rest and a chat, to get set for the endless work ahead. Cowroast was a landmark.

On this first occasion we stopped to congratulate ourselves. 'Not bad. We're getting the hang of this lark. How do you feel, girl?'

'Tired, but really we are getting it taped, aren't we?'

'Yes, but you must stop hitting those bridge holes. You keep chipping lumps off them with your stem.'

'I know, Jimmy, and I can't understand it. I aim right at the middle and always seem to hit one side or the other.'

'Now for the level. You can go on the snubber along here. It's two or three miles before Marsworth Flight.'

'Oh my God—Marsworth! I'm terrified of that place. I'll never get around those bends. Must I go on the snubber? It's so lonely way back there.'

'Ah, but we get along much faster. And try to keep your bows out of my wake when you go back on to the snatcher. You follow in line, keep yourself off set and we'll do better. All ready?'

'Yep. I'm looking forward to a beer tonight, aren't you?'

'Yes. We'll make fast at the bottom of Mafas, opposite the pub. Cheers now.'

We separated, each to our own boat. This habit of saying 'Hullo' or 'Goodbye' used to amuse us, but it was strange how, though no great distance from one another, we were each isolated on our own boat. Once I had gone aboard and started the engine, conversation with Gay on the butty was impossible, and sign language alone practical. When, as now, she was going on the seventy-feet-long snubber, the distance between us was little short of fifty yards.

The summit stretch was beautiful. We boated through woods, and past farms where ducks and geese thronged the cut. Coots and moorhens half ran, half flew across the water ahead of us, while a heron stood quite still on the towpath as we went by.

However, this blissful kind of boating ended all too soon, and we arrived at Marsworth Flight to find all seven locks against us. Our first descent was nothing to boast about, and what a game those engineers had here! The pounds, on an average, are about 100 yards long, and the route meanders in a crazy pattern of tremendous bends. I made many mistakes even with power. Gay more or less ground her way around the bends, her stem striking lumps from the stone parapet. Marsworth is really difficult.

We tied up by the 'Ship Café' at 6.15. We were exhausted

but cheered. It had been a great day. Many locks had been passed, and our boating was improving.

After sprucing ourselves up a bit, we walked to the 'Red Lion', which was kept by a grand bloke, an ex-'Queen's' infantry officer, whom we had met while we were waiting for our boats and walking sections of the canal to learn the road. We had arrived here one day by car to study Marsworth Flight. We had wanted to park and later have sandwiches. The pub was shut. I knocked. Rodney Eills came to the door. I made my requests.

'Certainly. Of course. Damned pleasant of you to ask. Mostly they just park anywhere that suits them. Rather. We've always something to eat—sandwiches, pickled eggs, pickled onions. Right. See you on the way back.'

Later, in the bar, we had enjoyed some excellent bitter and good grub. He sold Aylesbury Brewery beers in those days, real beer, conditioned in an oak cask, not blown from a tin by carbon dioxide. We had a long talk with him, and stayed until closing time. 'See you again one of these days no doubt, and the best of luck to you.' He had stood outside his pub and waved to us as we drew away. We felt we had made our first friendship by the cut.

Now, in jerseys, with windlasses tucked about us, myself clean but unshaven, Gay immaculate, all made up, looking normal except for the sea boots and trousers, we walked into the attractive bar.

There he was, tall, unchanged, drying a tankard. He looked up as we entered. For a moment he stared. Then recognition came, and he smiled.

'Hullo, you two. Good evening. Welcome back to the "Lion". How's it going? You've made it I see.' He looked at our windlasses, which we were carrying not for affectation but from force of habit. Except at bedtime they were always upon us. If one put them down for a few minutes, they somethow got lost or fell into the bilges, or, worse, into the cut.

'Good evening. It's good to be back.' We all shook hands. Gay asked after his wife. 'She's in the back,' he said. 'Go and see her. She'll be pleased to have a chat about your experiences.'

'I will, but I want a drink first. I'll take it in with me.'

'What would you like?'

'Oh, a pint please, a pint of your grand bitter.'

'A pint!' Rodney was surprised.

'Rather. I do a man's job these days and drink a man's drink.' She laughed.

I don't think I even tasted my first pint. It wet things on the way down, but that was all. The second I did taste. Over the third I lingered, and after that I just enjoyed them one by one. We had a cheerful evening. The pub filled. Many Polish refugees who were living in the converted buildings of an old aerodrome nearby came in—a jolly crowd who seemed to be very much at home in the 'Red Lion'. Towards closing time they sang their national songs to the accompaniment of a violin and an accordion, and they made real music. Their singing was organized, controlled, harmonious.

Once again we said farewell to Rodney Eills and his wife, promising to return as soon as possible. Arm in arm, a little tipsily, we walked through the bitter air back to our boats. The cabin was beautifully warm. We had eaten well in the pub. All that was left to do was to make up the range. Then I remembered that I had not put the cork into the outlet of the cooling system. If it froze during the night, the freezing air would blow into the pipe, and possibly turn the water in the bends to ice. I climbed out into the keen air, crossed to the monkey boat and lowered myself into the engine-room. Not only did I bung up the outlet but I also lit a hurricane lamp, and stood it near the water pump.

* * * *

We were late getting under way in the morning, but felt in great form without hangovers. We filled our water-cans at the tap by the lay-by, and cast off. We had to move about cautiously, as the boats and locks were white with thick frost.

It was a lovely day, and except that we picked up an old motor tyre in our propeller, everything went well. We were amused at Fenny Stratford to see the famous Lock 22.

'What's all this about?' Gay stood looking at the water levels.

'I'm not sure, but I believe it was due to an error of the engineers. They dug from both ends, and met here only to discover that they were about nine inches out.'

'Well, how daft! All this work for nine inches.'

'It wasn't a bad effort, you know. This cut was made in 1805.'

'Maybe, but I wish they had been a few feet out. It's just that I resent working a lock in order to climb nine inches. It seems so silly.'

'Oh well, one of these days you must complain to Mr Telford and his colleagues Barnes and Jessop.'

'I will, just for fun. Where are they? In London?'

'No, in heaven.'

'Oh do stop talking rot. Come on. We've a long way to go if we're going to make Stoke tonight.'

From Fenny to Stoke Bruerne is about seventeen miles, with only one lock at Cosgrove; but before that we had to cross the River Ouse in the famous aqueduct near Wolverton. It was a strange feeling. From being cradled in the earth, the cut suddenly enters what one might call the lower half of a rectangular cast-iron pipe, and the water-level is only about a foot below the top lips of the pipe. Earth and country are gone. One is boating in air. Far below is the river, and if one stands, tiller in hand, and looks to right or left, one might, apart from the lesser speed, be in the open cockpit of an old-time aeroplane.

Here the boats seemed to wish to become truly airborne, and about the last thing one can do is to steer a straight course. I rather enjoyed this apparently crazy form of boating, but when poor Gay realized that she was water-borne high in the sky she was terrified. However, it doesn't last long, and, when I looked back for the last time to make sure she was still on her long lead and following, she was steering with her hip, mopping her face with one hand and crossing herself with the other.

From being airborne, we became mixed up with the railway lines. Wolverton seems to be just one great web of lines and mass of sheds. We passed the arm of the cut which goes down to Buckingham, and at 5.48 p.m. arrived at the bottom of the Stoke Bruerne Flight, only to find the gates padlocked. There are only seven locks in this flight, and at the top are a village and a small pub right alongside the towpath, and a person we looked forward to meeting — the famous, beloved 'Sister Mary'. We bellowed and looked around, but there was not a sign of any living creature. The lock-keeper had evidently decided on an early evening and locked up twelve minutes before time. At about 6.30 we heard the sound of a pair. They had come down the flight, only to find themselves locked in at the bottom. This steerer and I had a yarn, and agreed that we held similar, and far from flattering, opinions of lock-keepers.

At 6 the following morning the engine of the locked-in pair started up. I walked to the lock, and was in time to catch the keeper, who had just removed the chain. He was surly and indignant. He assured me that my watch was wrong and that the gates were never chained before time.

Soon after the Stoke Flight came the infamous 3,050 yards of Blisworth Tunnel, and, although both of us had had the small experience of Maida and Islington which are unpleasant, we found Blisworth, one of the longest, absolute hell. Dante would perhaps have enjoyed the passage and gained inspiration for his *Divine Comedy*.

Someone had advised me to try closing my eyes before entering. I did, and nearly piled the boat into the bank just at the entrance. Regaining control, I aimed the bows at the oval hole, and in we went. The noise was painful, and very soon my eyes began to water. It became pitch dark. I switched my headlight on, but the beam seemed to resent the place also. It didn't penetrate. It was like using raised headlights in a fog. The cavern was all dank and smelly. The walls suppurated their particular kind of nastiness, and for the second time in two days I felt that we had left our rightful element. One could hardly believe that one was boating. It seemed more that one was standing on a trembling platform, grasping things which vibrated. One was trapped in a weird inferno of bitter air, and one moved slowly forwards through noise, along some wet brown intestine, into the very bowels of the earth.

Soon appalling things began to happen. Somewhere distant, up for'ard, my bows hit the wall. With a protesting noisy anguish the boat shook, and I moved the tiller over to bring her off. Then the stern crashed into the wall, and again she flexed and trembled. Once more I tried to straighten her, but I must have over-corrected, for again the bows hit. There was almost a devilish rhythm about this wild career. We were tacking through the tunnel. I cut the throttle right back, slowed almost to a stop and began all over again. For a while things went better, and ahead I could see some light coming down through the roof, and this made steering easier. No one had told me about the chief characteristic of these ventilation shafts. As we passed below I looked up, and, as if the Devil himself were above and playing tormenting tricks on his prey, a shower of water landed smack on my face.

For a moment I could see nothing. Shoving the tiller between my legs, I mopped the water from my eyes, ears and neck. Next I was almost overboard. The bows had once more struck the wall, and the whole boat lurched.

After well over half-an-hour of this incarceration, we rounded a curve, and there ahead was the small, white exit, which grew gradually larger as the minutes passed. I aimed my stem at the middle of it. It cheered me. It was a brick-framed picture of still life, fresh air and the countryside.

To the right was Gayton Junction, where an arm turns away northwards towards Northampton and the river Nene. We were now in a twelve-mile pound heading for the Buckby Flight and Norton Junction, where the canal divides again, one arm going north to Leicester, Loughborough and the river Trent, and the other westwards towards Birmingham. We 'turned left' as Gay would have it, and moored that night in Braunston after fighting through another 2,000 yards of tunnel.

We pulled out at about 7 next morning, and were soon well on our way along the five-mile stretch of the Oxford Canal. At Napton Junction we forked right, and were back again on the old Grand Union Canal. All this is now only a matter of names, for long ago this short section became part of the trunk route of the G.U. from Birmingham to London. Here the country opened out, but the cut went crazy, curving around endless bends towards the excellent new locks at Calcutt known as Wigram's Three.

From here onwards was a whole series of downhill locks, which lowered the boats 146 feet in seven miles, all of a new pattern and, by comparison with the normal type, very efficient. They were naked and characterless, but for us who were trying to earn a living most acceptable. So we fled through Itchington Ten, Bascote Four, Fosse Six and into the outskirts of Leamington, where a girl on the towpath winked at me, sang, 'I'd like to get you on a slow boat to China', and I think was really being a bit saucy about our progress.

To the people of Leamington we would have liked to address

a lecture, to tell them that the heart of this town was very pleasant but that it was more than time for them to look to their back yards, and the habits of those who lived there. We had to force our way along a canal choked with rubbish, past miles of appalling slums, through an atmosphere laden with the stink of gas. The backs of that Spa were a disgrace, and, to add to our troubles, someone had been felling trees along the embankment to the west of the town, and the cut was a mass of large branches.

From this rubbish dump we gladly passed to the start of the final climb upwards through Capes Two, and soon were at the foot of the hair-raising Hatton Twenty-One, which lifts the boats over a hill 150 feet high. The very thought of Hatton had for a long time depressed us. All on the cut talked of the toil up the 'Twenty-One', and now at last we had arrived. As Cowroast is a landmark, so is Hatton. One bides awhile below this fantastic flight, gazes aloft and tries to summon sufficient strength, and will, to begin the climb. Above, we were told, is a mental hospital, from which some of the inmates during clement weather come to help boaters work their boats. As we stood, aghast, at the foot of this giant's staircase, we felt that the hospital must surely be filled with canal folk who had found the strain too great.

We smoked our cigarettes and looked in awe at this magnificent but overpowering sight. I remarked, 'You must admit there's never a dull moment, or at least day, in this boating business.'

'Oh sure. Yesterday we were in hell, and now, by the look of that lot, we're off to heaven. What's the time?'

'Three-thirty. Do you feel like packing up, or shall we have a go?' I myself was quite willing to call it a day and start on this impossible-looking thing in the morning.

'Hell, Jimmy, we can't stop so early.'

'O.K., I was only thinking of you.'

And then she made her famous quotation, which ever afterwards, although frequently repeated, always made us laugh. She raised a hand above her eyes as if looking out across a sun-drenched sea, gazed towards the summit of the Twenty-One and said, 'I see no ships; only bloody hardships'.

Laughing, we breasted-up the pair, and began the great climb.

1 'Our butty was ready, complete with extra cabin'

Sheeting loaded boats in Regent's Canal Dock

2
'Keep yourself offset and we'll do better'

Aqueduct over River Ouse near Wolverton.
'Earth and country are gone, one is boating in air.'

3 Loaded monkey boat entering Braunston Tunnel

'There it was ahead of us: cranes, lorries, sheds, warehouses and dumps'

4 A loaded butty in the lock at Hawkesbury Stop

'In the pounds the noise was terrible as our metal hulls tore the solid surface apart'

5 Cowley Lock. 'A pair was in the lock heading up-country which meant work'

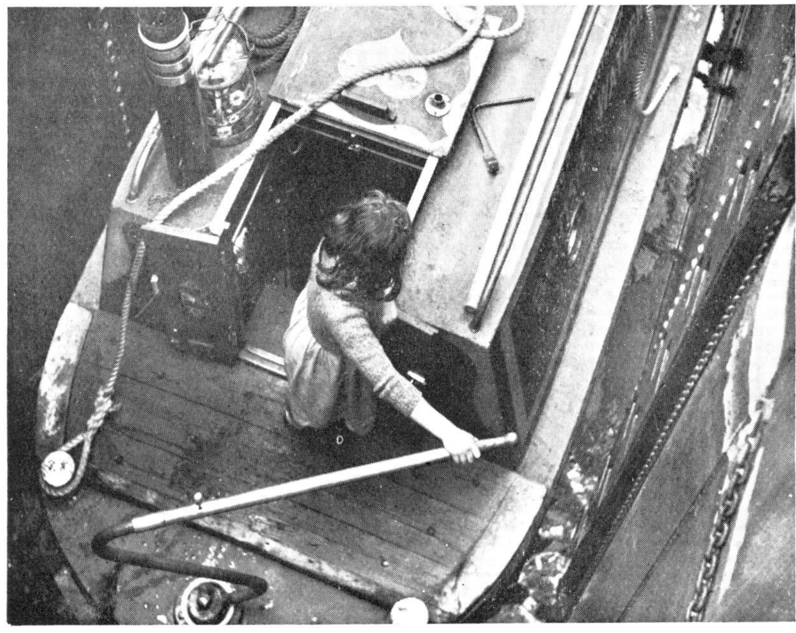

'They cannot even read!' A ten-years-old boater's daughter alone at the controls of a monkey boat as it enters a lock.'

6 'Let us enjoy our simple pleasures: our castles and roses, our brass, our painted cans'

'If he gets worse push on up to Stoke Bruerne and have Sister Mary look at him'

'Did Hatton in two hours which suggests we almost *are* boaters'

'I noticed Phelps walking towards us carrying a most beautifully painted and brand new Buckby water-can'

8 Pairs passing with captains concentrating on the correct positioning of their boats

The flight of locks at Knowle near Birmingham

We ran, wound, brought along the boats. Then we ran again and wound again. These new locks, though so smooth and dapper by comparison with their rugged elders, needed twice the number of turns of the windlass fully to raise the paddles.

Three hours later, completely whacked, in darkness, exalted by the conquest of the Hatton peak, we lowered ourselves slowly into the butty cabin, where the dear kettle was singing her welcome. Again I reached towards the medical stores, brought forth the rum bottle, waved it languidly at Gay and said, 'Yes?' In a quiet and happy voice she replied, 'Rather. And do remember to buy another bottle in Brum. I think it should be entered under "fuel" accounts, don't you?'

Again we slept that wonderful sleep which comes from physical exhaustion, exposure to fresh air, and a sense of achievement. By 5.30 next morning we were having breakfast. By 7 we were licking along the eight-mile pound towards the final flight of five locks at Knowle, boating through crisp cold air across a beautiful countryside.

Now a mere flight of five seemed as nothing. Almost scornfully we worked through these, and began the last lap of six-and-a-half miles to Tyseley Wharf, excited by the feeling of making the final spurt to the finish. Quite suddenly we left the countryside, and there the wharf was ahead of us — cranes, lorries, sheds, warehouses and dumps, all on a large expanse at a low level which enabled us to step ashore easily and watch all the activity of the place. Few boats were alongside. We drew in by an idle crane, and made fast. We were 150 miles from Limehouse, and the journey had taken us five-and-a-half days.

CHAPTER V

Coal for London

'Shall I go and tell them we're here, Jimmy?'

'They probably know.'

'Yes, but if I report we might be unloaded more quickly.'

'Good idea. You do that. I'll clean the boats.'

She walked across the wharf and into the office where a young man, seated behind a littered desk, talked into a telephone. She stood by a chair. He looked towards her eventually, smiled, clamped his hand over the blower and said, 'Oh, have a chair. Just hold on a minute, and I'll be with you.' Gay sat. He smiled some more, finished his conversation, left the phone and asked, 'What can I do for you?'

'I've brought a load of steel billets. Can we be unloaded soon, please?'

'*You* have? You on that pair?'

'Yes, "Chiswick" and "Bawtry", our boats'; then, proudly, and untruthfully, 'We're Number Ones, you know'.

'Good God. Things on the cut are looking up.'

'The trouble is getting loaded and unloaded quickly. Could you arrange a quick unloading for me?'

Again he said, 'Hold on a minute. I'll go and see how things are out there.' He left his office, and returned in a few moments whistling and said, 'I can't do anything about it this afternoon, but we'll start first thing tomorrow morning. You should be away by ten. How's that?'

'Oh great, and thanks. We'll clean up and go into Birmingham.'

'You'll find that exciting—I don't think.'

She came back to the boats where I was writing up the log:

05.15 hrs.	Rise.
07.35 „	Cast off from Hatton Top.
13.22 „	Moored Tyseley Wharf, Brum.

Analysis

5 hrs. 47 mins. 17 miles. 5 locks.
Average 2·9 m.p.h.

Remarks

The bridge-hole immediately above Knowle locks is a proper bastard. We struck something hard and must have nearly ripped our bottom.

Load

Steel billets 47½ tons.

Rate

10/- per ton.

Into Kitty

£23 5 0.

'Wow, goody. Twenty-three lovely pounds. Let's go and celebrate.'

'Yep, come on. I've made the boats look beautiful. Now for us. How's the kettle?'

'All ready. I'll wash first because I've got to put a face on and try to do something with my hands and what's left of my nails. The man in there doesn't seem to think we'll like Brum.'

'Oh, why not?'

'He didn't say. Only sniffed about it.'

'Talking of sniffing, Gay, there's an awful pong in this boat.'

'Isn't it you, dear?'

'Don't be so rude. Of course it isn't.'

'Oh well, not to worry, eh? We'll see how it is when we've washed.'

I was ashore before she was ready, and walked around trying to become used to wearing a shirt, tie and jacket again. Ahead of us was another pair with a young woman seated on the cabin top swinging her pretty legs to and fro in the steering well. She had watched us arrive and gazed while I cleaned down our boats. Now she looked again but at a body cleaned and smartly dressed. She laughed and called out, 'Oh I say, what a smasher!' Then out stepped Gay looking very neat and so attractive that even I had to take a second peep. That this could be the person who a few hours back had slaved up Hatton seemed impossible, and, although it was only about a week since she had dolled herself up for London's West End, the days had seemed months.

Our progress across the wharf was almost royal, and I felt as if I were accompanying a female V.I.P. Cranes ceased to work. Wolf whistles shrilled. Two lorry-drivers gave her the old signal on their hooters. An elderly stevedore called out, 'Eh, miss, you have left somethink be'ind.' Gay, laughing, called, 'Have I? What?' He, to the great admiration of his mates who burst into guffaws, answered, 'What? Me o' course.' The young man shot from his office to explain all about the buses and stops. In fact Tyseley enjoyed the first visit for some time of a London mannequin and film actress.

Gay was impolite about her reception. 'Silly lot of buggers, aren't they, really?' And somehow, although her usage of the word seemed normal on the cut, now that she was ashore, and rigged for town, it was quite shocking.

We had to wait at the bus stop, and again I noticed an awful smell in the air. 'Phew! What a dreadful stink around here,' I remarked, and Gay replied, 'Don't be so damned rude. It's not a stink. It's Lizzy Arden's "Blue Grass". Don't you really like it?'

I sniffed around her neck. 'Blimey, that's quite different. Oh yes, that's fine. But it's not that I can smell. Take a whiff, and see if you get it.' She breathed deeply, casting her nose around, and answered, 'Yes. Pooh! I hadn't noticed it before. Whatever can it be? It's not me, and, if you notice it, it probably isn't you. So it must be Tyseley.'

Eventually we learned about this smell and were surprised. That anything so pleasant could produce such a hum in the making was really astonishing. The smell issued from a very high chimney over the local Smith's Crisp factory, and always, while in Tyseley, we hoped the wind would veer, but it rarely did.

The City of Birmingham left us cold, wandering in dull streets in a kind of deadly darkness. Nothing seems, outwardly, to happen in Brum during the late evening. Nothing beckoned us. Nowhere cheered. We walked down ringing steps into cavernous pubs by tile-hung walls, and Gay remarked, 'It's more like going into a public lavatory.' These pubs were dead. The streets were empty. Our steps echoed in an abandoned town. From feeling cheerful and intending to celebrate, we quietened. Our bubble pricked, we sought a bus homewards, and jumped off at a vast pub before we reached Tyseley. We had seen some lights and distinctly heard music. We entered this place. The doors clanged to behind us and there was silence. The music must have been coming from somewhere else.

This pub, the biggest I had, or yet have, ever been in, was an expensively built and ornately decorated horror—a cathedral of a boozer, as empty and cold as many cathedrals are. Somewhere within someone was chanting, for the murmur of unseen voices wafted across the spaces. We stood at a bar before rows of glittering glasses and colourful bottles, and began to whisper to one another, for to laugh, or speak loudly, in such a place was surely irreverent. At last an ugly, tall, thin woman appeared —a phony blonde wearing thin metal-framed spectacles. She had no chest, no shape anywhere. Her body was in black silk, beads tight round her scraggy neck, her hands and nails dirty. She had no smile, no welcome, just 'Yes?'

We purchased two bottles of rum and two halves of bitter, which was very tasty stuff in fine condition. Quickly we sank the beer, and fled back to the wharf and our boats.

'Is this what they call the Black Country?' Gay asked.

'Not sure, but it gives me the blues. Pity. I hoped to celebrate, but isn't it good to be back? I love these cabins. One steps down here from towpaths or wharves, shuts the doors, pulls the hatch over, and suddenly one is home. Do you feel like that about them too?'

'Yes. I like the little range and the warmth in here and that great big spring mattress. Thank goodness we decided to invest in that. I don't think sleep has ever been so important, or so much appreciated. What's on the buzz box?'

I switched our portable on and found some good jazz. We changed into pyjamas, cooked sausages, eggs and bacon, and drank rum. We celebrated aboard, and enjoyed quite a party.

By 9.30 next morning both our boats were empty. The blokes who worked on them were cheerful and efficient. Whereas loading had been hell, the unloading went along quietly and swiftly. These fellows took just ten minutes more over the job, caused us no anxiety, did no damage to the boats, and cracked jokes with Gay about her changed appearance.

We winded the boats and were on our way back towards Hatton by eleven, having decided to go the long way round to Hawkesbury Stop, where we would receive orders for the coalfields. The infamous 'Bottom Road', with all its filth and single locks, is no road for a two-handed pair, so we tore along the route by which we had come, and tied up that night in Leamington, having travelled twenty-four miles through twenty-eight locks. At night the back of this town looked grimier, and stank even more of gas.

An early start next morning, and a crazy dash through the new locks brought us back to Braunston, where we turned left and began our journey up the Oxford Canal, passing through Hillmorton's three locks into a pound fifteen miles long. Eventually, late at night, bitterly cold and again exhausted, we arrived at Hawkesbury Stop, having boated thirty-seven miles and worked twenty-seven locks.

At nine the following morning we reported at the Control Office to a most charming person, who listened to my worries about stacking a fair load on the butty, immediately rang a friend of his in Charity Dock, and arranged for the quick making of two ten-feet slack boards to be picked up as we passed that afternoon. Our orders were to load coal at the wharf by Atherstone Top Lock, for delivery to Yeading Dock near Hayes Road, Southall.

As we had some time to waste, we ambled around Hawkesbury, looked into the windows of the pub, and visited the shop. We laughed about the lock, which either raised or lowered the boats only a few inches, and studied the method of taking a pair around the apparently impossible hairpin bend beyond the basin.

Then I spotted a very special pair of boats belonging to the Samuel Barlow Coal Company — M.B. 'Cairo' and butty 'Warwick', crewed by Mr and Mrs Smith. We had read and heard a lot about Sonia Smith. She had come to the cut during the war when many pairs were crewed by fit young girls, some of them yachtswomen, all wanting to do something practical to help the war effort. Kit Gayford, a copy of whose famous map we used daily, was one; Sonia was another. The Press had got hold of Sonia's story. Her picture appeared in numerous papers under such headings as 'The Queen of The Cut', 'Champion of the Boaters', 'Sonia Takes Over the Helm'. Then followed a load of balderdash about sailors who never saw the sea, women who steered 'barges', and so on.

Sonia must have liked the life, for she married a boater, and stayed on the cut, and here she was in Hawkesbury. We knocked on the butty cabin, and for the next two-and-a-half hours were talking shop with them. They came to see our extra cabin. From them we learned a number of tips. In fact we had a good yarn together — Gay and Sonia on the female angle, George and I discussing practical matters which immediately concerned boating and the cut. After parting, we felt we had made our first friends among the boaters, and looked forward to meeting them again some evening when we would have a session in a cut-side pub. But, strangely enough, though we frequently saw them, never did we both tie up at the same place again.

We worked our way round the famous bend without making too much of an exhibition of ourselves, collected our slack boards, and winded the pair below Atherstone Top, bringing them alongside a small open space where there was neither crane nor office.

'Do you suppose this is where they mean? I was expecting to find a busy wharf,' I remarked.

'There's coal dust around here.'

'While I clean the boats you had better go and ask some questions. This place doesn't look right to me.'

She was soon back. 'It's here. We're right. They tip it in from lorries. See those galvanized sheets there?'

'Yes.'

'Well those go between the edge of the bank and our gun'ales. They back up and shoot the coal down them into the holds.'

'Who told you all this?'

'Oh, a white-haired lady I met. She says it's grand because half of it goes into the cut, and, when we leave, the locals pour from these cottages and hook it out with special forks.'

'No wonder coal is so expensive.'

'We must bunker up, Jimmy. My old lady says it's really good stuff.'

We walked around the town, had a few excellent beers, caused something of a stir in most of the pubs we visited, and went early to bed.

We had our boats ready by 8.30 a.m. The holds were cleared, the top planks stacked out of the way, and the first load already overdue. By 11.30 I was mad with rage, and Gay had gone off to find a telephone and talk to the Boat Control Officer. He, good man, said he was pleased she had let him know of the delay. He would phone the colliery. Would she stay in the box until he rang back? He was through fairly soon, and said loading would start immediately after lunch. The colliery office did not know we were there—in spite of the fact that we had been ordered to be ready by 8.30 a.m.

At 3.10 p.m. a convoy of tippers arrived. Thirty-five minutes later we had 24 tons 16 cwt. on the motor-boat and 24 tons 8 cwt. on the butty. We had waited seven-and-a-quarter hours. The whole business was a disgrace, and, though I couldn't estimate the quantity which fell into the cut, it certainly must have been a matter of hundredweights.

However, one thing pleased me. The slack boards were a great success. We had forty-nine tons aboard, and the boats trimmed well. In fact, we could certainly have taken more on the butty. It was good to know that the extra cabin was in no way going to reduce our loads of coal or other heavy cargoes.

Now the serious business of delivering our load began again. As always, we worked from first light until dark, went early to bed and seldom left the boats unless there was a pub right by our mooring place. We began each trip with a fully-stocked larder and made small purchases in the numerous canal shops which often were also pubs, otherwise in little general stores, which had come into being in the great and busy days before the railways strangled the waterways.

Our journey back to Hawkesbury was uneventful, and unattractive. The land rose sharply along the right side of the cut. The water was a filthy black sort of soup. The bridge-holes were cluttered with rubbish and we bumped our way through them. Most repulsive, the stretch was the graveyard of dogs. It was January, licence time. In eleven miles I counted eight drowned dogs, which had been murdered by their owners—tied in weighted sacks or thrown into the canal with weights roped to their collars.

Apart from our tasks at the gauging lock where the Coventry Canal joins the Oxford in Hawkesbury Basin, we had no work to do all day. It was just a matter of steering, and, as the temperature had dropped to freezing, we stiffened at our tillers. Gay was better off than I, as the range in the butty gave her some warmth. As we moved along hour after hour, she crept further and further towards the top of the steps which led down into the cabin. I envied her. There was no steering cockpit on the motor-boat. One stood fully exposed on a flat counter, and I had not lighted the range.

Mile followed mile of twisting cut through open country, and the banks along the stretch were so eroded and trampled by cattle that it looked more like a small river than a canal. Our aim was to moor at Hillmorton, below the locks, but that place seemed to have disappeared from the land. Darkness came, and on we went, our headlights sweeping the countryside, searching for this flight of three locks. Our hands, cramped and curved, froze to the tillers. I could not feel my feet. Yet, apart from this extreme discomfort, it was a fascinating experience. The engine turned with a steady, friendly, familiar, rhythmical beat. The exhaust note, to one who cared for engines, was musical. Water careered gaily out of the meadows as we drew it, and backed up again as we passed, splashing with excitement at our coming. In the distance, lights shone from farm and cottage windows. Here and there long flat lines of light flew through the countryside ahead of some speeding car.

Then, suddenly, my light focused on two great trunks of timber, white-tipped, balanced, pointing to right and left, resting on top of a large black gate. We had arrived after eleven-and-a-half hours of steering along twenty-seven miles of meandering water.

We awoke to a white world—not snow but such a frost that the cut was covered with a thin layer of ice. The first thing I did was to light the range in the monkey boat's cabin, for there was not going to be any repetition of yesterday's discomfort. At first light we were all set to start. I went across, grasped the great thick snatcher with which we moored the boats, and pulled. Absolutely nothing happened. The rope was like metal, a great bar of brown metal forged into the shape of knots. I had to use a long-handled four-pound hammer to undo that frozen thing, while Gay poured hot water from the kettle around the bends.

This was only the beginning of a trouble-filled day. The next snag was that the lock gates were frozen together, and it took us quite a time and a great expenditure of brute force to open them. We had begun the day clothed in layers of jerseys and pullovers. Now we were in a sweat, almost steaming. Hillmorton's are single locks, allowing the passage of only one boat at a time. I boarded the monkey and, for some reason we never understood, Gay came also. I put the boat into gear, and, fortunately, opened the throttle only slightly. She crept into the lock, and, as we were passing the parapet at the foot of the steps up the lock, Gay jumped for it. She landed, slipped, regained her footing, leaned over backwards, and for apparently quite a long time waved both her arms in circles as if she was warming herself up. Then, giving a most dreadful scream, she toppled bottom first into the cut. Swiftly I abandoned ship also, and arrived at the spot by the time she came up, grabbed hold of her and heaved. She came out of the cut almost more quickly than she had entered, and apart from her legs and feet—her trousers had leaked—was quite dry inside. The water had not had time to percolate the layers of wool.

This accident, which might have been serious, put us on the alert, and for the remainder of that day, and many days to come, we moved about slippery locks and boats mighty carefully.

After all this excitement we left Hillmorton, and, apart from some peculiar steering of the butty nothing went wrong until we reached the Braunston Flight. Here I got into serious trouble with a well-known and heartily-disliked pair of steerers. There are laws about working locks in flights. If one is going up and sees a pair coming down, one does not begin to work the next lock to the one in which they are resting. It is their lock, and one waits. Well, I didn't even see this pair at the time. They were well down in their lock and almost out of sight, or I would certainly have spotted them. I always made a point of treating boaters with the greatest courtesy.

Quite accidentally I pinched their lock and kept them waiting. As our boats passed in a pound, the steerer of the monkey began pouring a really terrible flood of oaths in my direction, and ended by screaming, 'What yer do it for, yer silly bastard?'

I didn't intend to explain. I hadn't time anyway, as our boats were swiftly passing in opposite directions. Instead I cupped a hand around my ear, and leant in his direction as if unable quite to hear his question. Again, but this time punctuated by far worse coarseness, he repeated the question. I remained quiet, hand cupped. Now I was nearing his mate, who began a speech simply crammed with obscenities. But then the for'ard steerer called, ' 'Tis no bleedin' use, Alf. The bugger's deaf as well as f . . . in' blind!'

We passed through Braunston Tunnel, down Buckby Flight and into the sixteen-mile pound between there and Stoke Bruerne. But there was further trouble to come. We entered the Blisworth intestine, and were feeling our way along the soggy walls when, much to my horror, I saw a light ahead of us, and realized that a pair was approaching. The first time this happens it is a frightening experience. To begin with, it looks quite impossible for boats to pass. One has the feeling that no other person would ever venture into such a hell of a place. And finally one's boats seem to take charge, and refuse to go or stay where one aims them.

I cut the throttle, and immediately Gay and the butty, which has no kind of brakes, rode up on me. I thought of the great long snubber lying curled on the bottom of the cut, just waiting its opportunity to rise and seize hold of someone's prop. I began heaving it in and decided not to worry about my bows, but to leave the oncoming steerer to shove them over when he reached them. As I was hauling he arrived, struck us a sound smite up for'ard, and nearly shot me into the water. On he came, and up astern of me the butty bows loomed. I hitched the snubber, now just a short length, on to a stud, and, trampling on yards of uncoiled wet rope, reached for the throttle, opened it slightly, and moved ahead.

Our boats ground past one another. As the other steerer moved by he bawled, 'How d'you do?' And I, trying to look as if in complete control, a cool, polite fellow, answered rather foolishly, 'Oh, I'm fine thanks. And you?' which surprised the fellow exceedingly. I was still laughing to myself about my fatuous remark when the boat was struck another and even fiercer blow by the butty he was towing. I decided to be ready to pass the time of day with the steerer of this boat. I watched its hold and its lighted cabin go by, and there, tiller in hand, glaring in my direction, stood an elderly woman. She had a wrinkled face, a plait of hair across her forehead, sleeves rolled above massive arms, ear-rings dangling. 'How d'you do?' I bellowed.

'Why don't cher keep yer bleedin' front over? Oh. Might have guessed. One of they trainees!' Refusing to take offence, I immediately waved to her, and she floated away into the darkness smiling and waving.

It was dusk when we entered the tunnel, and dark when we came out, but immediately ahead was Stoke Bruerne, and we tied up near the mouth of the top lock. Soon we were down under, doors closed, lights and radio on, and our old friend the kettle purring away.

'How do you feel after your ducking? All right?'

'Oh yes. I didn't get all that wet anyway, and I knew I was going in, so it wasn't any sort of shock. What worried me was the thought of the prop.'

'You were lucky. If you'd jumped sooner you might have been chopped up. Now no more silly leaping around, and remind me to have your boots studded. It would help.'

'You made some mess of passing that pair in Blisworth, didn't you?' She laughed.

'Well, maybe, but it was a first experience. What were you doing all the time?'

'Oh I just came down here and let them go by.'

'Good God! You quit? Did nothing?'

'Certainly! Why not? That was all I could do when you come to think about it.'

'Incidentally,' I said, trying to score a point, 'your steering this morning was terrible. You hit at least six bridges.'

'Oh I know. Bridge holes have me foxed any time, but all this morning I felt as tight as a coot. You gave me all that rum, after I fell in. Remember? It's nice. I like it. But as I came from the warm cabin after changing, into the bitter air, it hit me a fearful bank, and the blasted bridge holes wouldn't stay still.'

'That was it! I thought you'd lost your nerve or something. What a woman you are. You take fright in tunnels and hide in the cabin. You leap through ice into the cut, and are drunk in charge of a seventy-feet boat—all in one day. Quite disgusting! Kettle's boiling. Shall we have a shot of rum in our tea?'

'Oh goody, yes. I've decided I'm partial to rum.'

* * * *

It was a white world again next morning, and we had a hell

of a game trying to break open the gates of the Stoke flight. The lock-keeper helped us all the way, and explained some tricks for working boats in a frozen canal. Before we could take the pair into a lock, all the broken ice had to be scooped out, or it jammed everywhere. Progress was slow, and our hands frozen from lifting sheets of the stuff and slinging it away into fields. In the pounds the noise was terrible as our metal hulls tore the solid surface apart, and it scraped along our sides. Later the sun came out. The day was beautiful, but still the water froze. We ground our way along to Fenny, worked through the nine-inch lock and tied up just below it.

We decided to pack up early. Our faces ached. Our teeth ached. We, too, were almost frozen stiff. Quite a few boats were made fast already, and the steerer of a wooden pair told us he had not moved for the day, and wouldn't dare to in ice as thick as that, for it would cut his hull to ribbons.

Right by the lock was one of the wonderful pubs one finds along the cut. In Fenny no man grumbles at being asked to go shopping, for, with a pint in one hand, it's but a step to examine the potatoes, select a cabbage, choose the tinned soups. If, when one returns to the boats, something, as is most likely, has been forgotten, it doesn't take a minute to nip back for another pint and complete the list.

We cleaned up after supper, and went across to the pub, which was quite full, mainly with boaters. Some of them we knew by sight, having seen them either in the depôt lay-by or along the road. As we approached the counter, one turned and said, 'How d'you do? How you going along?' We recognized Herbert Chitty, and were delighted to see him. Yarning with Chitty brought us into the family of boaters, for mostly they were still shy of us, and conversation was limited to passing the time of day.

'We're going fine, thanks. Just on our third trip.'

'What have you got on then?'

'Coal,' I replied, 'from Atherstone for Yeading.'

'What she take, that butty of yours?'

'24.8 on the butty.'

'Down fore end I should say.' This remark came from the man alongside Chitty. I looked at him to answer, and remembered his face immediately—Steerer Phelps. We had marked him long ago when he had passed our boats on his way to answer a call from the P.A. in the depôt office. Again later, in Brentford Dock, he had been among those who helped us to make fast after my phenomenal display of winding.

'No, not now. We have ten-feet slack boards along the back end, and we load her high there first of all.'

Chitty turned to Phelps, and said, 'Not a bad load for a butty with all that took out of the 'old. Worth it I'd say. You been aboard then?'

'No, just seen her.'

' 'Tis what you and your missis needs with they two kids of yours. Missis here would show you. Wouldn't you, me dear?'

'Oh yes, certainly. Any time.' Gay was surprised to be suddenly brought into the conversation, and remarked, 'But I don't know your wife, Mr Phelps. Is she here?'

'Aye, yonder with me daughter. Come on over.'

They moved away to the far side of the bar, where all the wives were together, talking away at a deuce of a rate and laughing merrily. I watched them go towards a table where, among others, sat a good-looking, frail, short, middle-aged woman and a handsome girl with a high forehead, light complexion and shoulder-length fair hair. Both of them were well turned out, and scrubbed clean. They looked the type who were proud of themselves, and one could guess that their boats also would be smart. Phelps introduced Gay to them and returned.

Chitty and I were talking. 'That's your woman settled. They'll have some cackle, I'll be bound,' Phelps said.

Chitty continued, 'No, 'tis so different now. I reckon all hope for the cut finished when the Number Ones were driven off. So many of the young 'uns don't care, and all the damage to boats and locks don't matter. They haven't got to pay for it.'

Phelps said, 'We had hopes when nationalization come. But nothing's happened 'cepting they can't afford to paint the boats proper. Saved a few quid a pair it did, and all our painting gone. They was nice before, all colour, and we liked some colour around. We ain't got no gardens, see.'

'I remember,' Chitty said, 'when they was diamonds, squares and roses almost all over. It was people like Nurser and Tooley could turn out a boat.'

'To me,' I said, 'it seems that overhanging trees and lack of dredging are the two biggest snags. There was so much talk about our extra cabin reducing the load, but if you loaded more than 50 tons on your own boats you'd have trouble. It's not a matter of what they might hold. It's the problem of no water, no depth.'

'True enough,' said Chitty, and laughing added, 'I would like, Jim, to see you going through the parks with 55 ton.'

'Booger me, but I wouldn't! What gets me is to see 'em cutting the hedges nice and neat, and, while I'm watching, a bloody great branch of a tree swipes me chimley off.' Jim Phelps laughed heartily.

I asked them, 'Did you ever work boats with horses?'

'I'll say,' Phelps replied.

'Oh bless you, yes,' said Chitty. 'But we was too slow then, so they gave us engines. I've seen Joshers steam-driven, but me first was a Bolinder. What a lark it was too. She had hot spots, and we used a blowlamp to get her started. Ever had a Bolinder, Jim?'

'No, Herb. Nationals all the time, me.'

'Bolinders was all right once you got them started. Almost see the one big cylinder going up and down, so slow it was. And when she fired it near shook you off the bloody counter. Vibration, cor! Shake you like jelly.'

'Too slow you say. Now all the engines are governed down because we goes too fast,' Phelps remarked.

Chitty looked at him as if surprised, and said, 'Strike me. You know how to fix that surely.'

Jim winked. 'I've got an idea.'

Gay came back with Mrs Phelps and introduced me to her and her daughter, Violet. 'We're going across to see the boats, Jimmy. That's my tankard, but I don't want any more beer. I'll have a nice large rum when I come back. Bye.'

'Have a care out there. It will be slippery on the lock and the boats.'

'Don't worry. Once is enough.'

As they left I heard her say to Mrs Phelps. 'Yes, right in backwards.' And they all laughed together.

'How's missis doing then?' Chitty asked.

'Fine. She's good. Only trouble is she will hit bridge holes. I can't understand it.'

'I can. That's an old one.'

'What does she do wrong then?' I asked.

'Well, it's like this, see. You put your boat at the hole, in the middle, you think. But it never is—always a little to one side or the other. As you come on in, you push the water out down both sides of your fore end, but always more goes one side than t'other. It builds a bigger, heavier wedge, so over goes the fore end. Now a proper steerer sees that start, and counter-steers hard, which pushes the fore end over against the wedge, and in she goes lovely. That jannock, Jim?'

'Right enough. Your missis, Captain, waits too long. It's like instinct to see early which way she's going.'

'Incidentally, Mr Chitty, I have a bone to pick with you. What about all that cold water that pours down the ventilation shafts at Blisworth. You didn't warn us of that.'

'Look here, I'm Herbert, and this here's Jim. Let's have it that way now, shall us? Forget the Mister.'

'Oh, right. But I'm Jim, or Jimmy, too.'

'You're a Number One, mate, Captain will do for you. That's it. Captain Jim, and that makes two of them—there's Captain Bishop remember [the man I had first met at Berkhamsted]. Cut's looking up, eh, Jim?' Chitty dug Phelps in the ribs, and he replied, 'Aye, two of 'em! Should be two hundred, and then it would be a different place. See some stuff shifted then.'

'Would an' all. But, coming back, Blisworth got you then?'

'Right in the eye. I looked up the shaft to see the sky and convince myself I wasn't dreaming. What a hell hole it is!'

'It's nothing now,' Chitty said. 'In my time I've legged it, lying flat on the wings. It's nothing to be on about these days.'

Gay, Mrs Phelps and Violet returned. After a deal of argument I persuaded them—not Gay; she doesn't argue—to have a drink with me, and we stood in a group for a while chatting, as usual, about the cut. We talked about waiting to be loaded, about low pounds and ice—all things so important in a boater's life. Violet was very quietly spoken and painfully shy of me. Most of the time she just watched Gay, and smiled every time their glances met. Mrs Phelps was a lively, jolly soul, and she talked away, laughed and joked as freely with us as with Herbert and her man.

We left before closing time, and went home discussing the

pleasures of the evening. We were pleased at having broken ice not only in the cut that day, but also among its people.

'I felt awful when Phelps took me over to that table. But do you know, Jimmy, they all called me "me dear" or "dearie" and seemed to be genuinely interested in how we were going along. I've never answered so many questions in all my life.'

'Incidentally, Gay, Phelps thinks—in fact he is sure—that he could find us a really good third hand if we decide to take one.'

'Oh good! I do think it would be better, don't you?'

'Yes, but I must look into our accounts. We would have to pay him and feed him. He'd have the monkey-boat cabin to himself, and we'd have to shift all our gear out. Probably we could dump it in the depôt stores.'

'With three we could go fair bollocking along.'

'Don't say that! You must not use that word.'

'Well, you do. What's wrong with bollocking anyway? I don't even know what it means. What's it mean?'

'Forget it. It's not a word for a lady to use.'

'I'm no lady. I'm a boater. I bet Mrs Phelps knows. I'll ask her when we next meet.'

* * * *

Two days later we reported at Yeading Wharf, late in the evening. The man in charge, a happy kind of fellow, promised to begin unloading our boats first thing next morning. At 8.30 they started. By 9.20 the job was finished, and at 11 we were back in the lay-by at Bull's Bridge.

My first task was to bring the log up-to-date, and the final entries were:

Atherstone to Yeading Wharf.		127 miles.
Time on move.		56 hrs. 40 mins.
Total waiting times.		9 hrs. 35 mins.
Loading.		35 mins.
Unloading.		55 mins.
Cargo.	Coal.	
Tonnage.	49¼ tons.	
Rate.	11/7½d.	
Into kitty.		£28 12 6
Remarks.		

Gay in cut. Ice makes things difficult. Good party in Fenny. Jumped carelessly from lock on to cabin roof carrying two cans of water. Thought for a moment I had dislocated neck again. Jarred left shoulder badly. Bullet holes look O.K., but it hurts under pressure. Must take more care—both of us.

CHAPTER VI

Summing Up

DURING our first three months on the cut we completed nine trips carrying: coal (three cargoes), timber, scrap bullets, electro-copper wire bars, steel, meat powder and wood-pulp.

At the finish of the last trip, while we were having a few days' rest in the lay-by, Phelps came in, and we had a long natter on the subject of the pros and cons of three-handed boating. Our final decision was that, as well as providing a pleasant easier-going life, it was quicker and more efficient, and the saving in time would permit us to pack at least one more trip into each month.

The boy he had in mind came from an old family of boaters called Redknap. His name was John. He was seventeen years old, and one of a family of five living on a pair of boats. His younger brother was now fourteen, and already did a man's job on the boats. The father would like to see his eldest son move on to another pair and begin to earn his own living. This would leave more room for the parents, who could then put their remaining children in the monkey and have the butty to themselves.

'Do you think that Redknap would allow his son to come with us? I mean, we are what they call "trainees" and not very popular about the cut.'

'Oh, don't you think that. Not now. You and your woman have done a good job. That's all over. At the beginning they thought you was going to play around, be a nuisance like. But they don't think that any more.'

'I'm glad. We have been as careful as possible; kept out of their road and made the least of ourselves. But to us they still seem as if they suspected something. They aren't friendly.'

'At first you had enemies; said all sorts of you they did. Some told me you were police. Others said you were set to spy on them. You know how people go on, but when nothing horrible happened all that talk stopped. Then there's your woman and the others. They all think she's a bloody marvel, all 'cepting a few old ones, who say no decent woman ever wears trousers.'

'Oh well, perhaps, as time goes by, they'll become more pally.'

'They will, but you must talk to them. They're shy of you. We haven't got many like you to talk to. Now during the war, when all they girls was around, it was different, and the woman folk became used to people like your missis.'

'Well thanks, Jim, for your advice. Have you any idea what Redknap would expect us to pay his boy?'

'Ah, I meant to speak of that. He and I talked it over after our evening in Fenny. Remember? Amos hopes the boy might get his keep and a quid a week. That's what he hopes, mind.'

'A quid!' I exclaimed.

'Yes. Why, you reckon that's too steep?'

'Oh no. I thought it might be more, to be honest.' Then quickly to change the subject, because I had no wish to inflate wages on the cut, I asked him, 'One worry of mine is how to treat the boy if he should start playing the fool'.

'You'd bloody well leather him, same as his dad. That's how. Don't reckon though that you'd have any trouble. I can tell, just between you and me mind, he hopes you'll ask him. His dad is real keen for you to take him. Old Amos thinks you might teach the boy to read and write and make a real gentleman out of him.'

* * * *

Later I told Gay all this, and we sat down and wrote out our accounts in a page of the log book:

THE FIRST THREE MONTHS

9 trips		Carried	429 tons 16 cwts.		
Average load			47 tons 15 cwts.		
Consumed:	Fuel oil	539 galls. @ -/11¾	£26	7	10
	Lube. oil	2 galls. @ 4/-		8	0
	Paraffin	3 galls. @ 1/2		3	6
		Total	£26	19	4

Rent, 13 weeks	@ £2 weekly	£26	0	0
Insurance for boats etc.	@ £1 weekly	13	0	0
N.H. Stamps	@ 11/6 weekly	6	18	10
Grub	@ 30/- per head wkly.	39	0	0
Clothes kitty	@ 10/- per head wkly.	13	0	0
Personal	@ 50/- weekly	65	0	0
Total		£189	18	2
Receipts from loads		£214	6	0
Profit Balance	£24 7 10			

'Golly, that's damn all. Not even two quid a week!' She sounded disgusted, and I must admit that I was rather surprised.

'Ah, remember we took days off at Christmas, and we are only beginners. This is from scratch. We shall certainly improve on it.'

'Unloading is the trouble — those days doing nothing but waiting. Four days at Blisworth Wharf, three days at Warwick —there goes a week on two trips.' She looked downhearted.

I thought about the problem, and concluded that (a) we could not carry heavier loads, as the state of the cut made that impractical, (b) we could not work much harder than we had been doing, (c) as long as road-haulage was given precedence over boats at all docks and wharves, as it now was, we could do little to hasten loading or unloading except complain. The answer then was a third hand, who would help us to move more quickly and work longer hours under less strain. If the cost of his small wage and subsistence was not more than covered by our increased efficiency, then, either our rates per ton must go up, or we must think again about the practicability of the business as an occupation.

I did not, much as I loved the life, intend to work so hard for so little profit. In our accounts nothing had been entered to cover emergencies. Our fifty-shillings-a-week pocket-money was about the only reserve, and we earned a smoke, a few beers, a cinema, theatre or concert seat now and again, and books were essential. Already the two shelves along the sides of our extra cabin were becoming furnished with colourful bindings and jackets. There was also the frightening possibility of some kind of breakdown in the engine or gearbox of the monkey boat. Our financial condition was unhealthy, and I felt that we must try three-handed boating.

Possibly with the longer days coming, and someone ashore lock wheeling, we might achieve a really worthwhile increase in speed, but I was rather haunted by the memory of our recent exertions and how, after taking risks and working ourselves to complete exhaustion, we were told on arrival at a wharf, 'There are three pairs ahead of you. We unload at the rate of a pair a day. Come back on Thursday, will you.' At one place it was, 'We have only one hoist, and that's broken. I can't say when you will be unloaded.'

At another, we could not bring the boats alongside, for lack of dredging, and there was no mechanical handling. This cargo was in cases. It was manhandled from the holds on to planks between wharf and boat, pulled across this watery gap by nervous casual labourers and lifted into a five-ton lorry. There were two lorries only on the job, and each had to travel some miles to unload and return to the wharf. One entry in the log reads:

Total time on the move	37 hrs. 45 mins.
Total time waiting around	72 hrs.

There was little we could do to alter these circumstances, but it struck me that it would help if I could squeeze some money from somebody to assist in paying my expenses while hanging around. I went to London, had a long talk to the Traffic Manager, who had all along been kind and helpful to us, and came away with the promise of £1 a day demurrage to start on the third day of waiting. Back on the boats I looked up this word 'demurrage' in my dictionary, and it said, 'Undue delay, detention, of vessels in port; compensation, allowance for this'. It all sounded grand, but in the future I was to discover that the only grand thing about it was the word. One pound a day did not go far either to cover our expenses or make up for lack of earning capacity.

After a lot of talking round the problem, we decided to employ John Redknap. His pair was traced by Mr Newbury, and a message passed to the boy by a lock-keeper. He appeared in the depôt lay-by the following day, and we had a long talk with him. The lad was decked out in his Sunday best—hair greased down, hands and nails cleaner than ours, shoes shining. He was short, slim, agile. When invited aboard, he didn't climb from the parapet into the cockpit. He seemed to spring from one to the other, and the speed of his movements was quite alarming.

He was shy and continually played with his fingers, head lowered, watching their movements. He assured me that *he* wanted to join us, and had not been pushed into the idea. He preferred steering the monkey because he liked engines. He was never ill, and he could join us immediately, or rather tomorrow, with all his gear. I told him to do that and said goodbye to him. He extended his hand. He shook, and I noticed the hardness and extraordinary size of his fist. It was large out of all proportion—no doubt from handling windlasses since he was a little nipper.

We set about the task of clearing and cleaning the monkey boat's cabin. Experience had taught us what we needed aboard. Everything else was packed and dumped in the depôt stores. By the following day that cabin had been scrubbed out, dried and polished. The range and its chimney shone. All the straps were white and neatly coiled. Every piece of brass or copper in the engine-room was highly polished. The engine block, water-pump, tanks—all had been cleaned of every spot of oil or grease. It looked magnificent, and that was how I wanted young John to find it, and intended that in the future he should keep it.

At the close of a busy day I went to see Mr Newbury to tell him that we were ready for orders. In the evening we returned to Richmond, wallowed in hot baths, and drank Young's beer in the 'White Cross' on the water-front with members of the family. They all said we were crazy, but nevertheless asked innumerable questions about our occupation. It seemed to us that, although they pretended that we had gone mad, they were rather jealous of the interesting and unusual life we were living.

Among the locals of the pub were a few old Thames longshoremen, who were truly excited to hear of our job. They remembered the good old days when narrow boats came up river from London, past this pub, and on up to Reading and the Kennet and Avon Canal, or Weybridge and the River Wey Navigation. To these longshoremen we became something of heroes, and there was nothing they liked more than to talk about our boats and journeys, our cargoes and exciting experiences.

Back on board that night we chatted late—of the future and

how greatly our life would be altered by the presence of a third hand. We would be together in one boat. We could have more reasonable meals during the day. Our tasks could be varied, whereas up to now we had both done the same things every day. And, lastly, we could claim our road, instead of giving way to three-handed boats, or even the many two-handed who could work that little bit more quickly than ourselves. All this giving way had meant that day after day the majority of the locks had been against us. With a better road, a third hand and some experience we'd show 'em. It would not be long before we would hold our own against all, and become as good boaters as any.

PART TWO

Spring

CHAPTER VII

Milk-Powder to Leicester

We sat on the butty. Gay was on the cabin top, on two coils of cotton side-straps, her hair resting on the head of a mop, looking upwards towards a warm sun. I was on the gun'ale, aft, looking along the wharf into the hold, where cases of milk-powder were being stacked.

Up and down walked an over-dressed gentleman wearing, of all incongruous gear, a bowler hat. He was sour-faced, unsmiling, watchful. On the hoist, in the hold, on the wharf, stevedores talked and laughed as they worked. The whole scene was cheerful, splashed with colour, warm, busy. We were at Brentford Dock in May. The sun was up; shirt-sleeves were up; bedding was out airing; blankets were up, basking in holds on bow-hauling-lines.

A few more hoists and our butty would be full. We could then sheet-up and make her shipshape for the long journey. The minute hand on the large clock jumped, shivered a moment, stilled. The clock showed five in the evening. The man under the bowler stuck a whistle in his mouth and blew a shrill blast. The stevedores rolled down their sleeves, reached for their coats and began to move away. There were only eight cases remaining to be stowed and the job could be finished in two more lifts.

Stepping from the butty I approached the whistler, smiled, and said, 'Look, mate. A couple or three minutes more and I could get sheeted-up. Let them put those few in—please.'

Contemptuously staring at me as if I were something revolting, he snarled, 'Bugger you', turned and walked away.

The shock was so great that it was a few seconds before I could speak. Then I called after him, 'I'll put the bloody things on myself'. The idea came to me that I would like to see this charming fellow floating down the cut underneath his stupid hat, and I added, bawling to make sure he heard, 'And keep moving, because, if I catch up with you, I'll sling you in the cut, mate'.

He stopped at this, and so did his gang. All turned to see the fun. 'You touch those,' he called, pointing at the poor little heap of cases. 'Just you touch those . . . ' I started after him, determined to smack his bowler down over his big ears. He turned about again, pushed his way through his buddies, and hastened down the wharf, leaving this threat unspoken. I followed, but slowed, all ideas of harming the little runt gone now that I had regained control of myself; but I intended asking permission at the office to stack the few cases aboard and get on with my sheeting. He looked back once, saw me closing on him, increased his speed until he was nearly running and disappeared behind a mountainous stack of drums.

In the office I told my story, and made my request. The fellow in charge said, 'God, man, whatever you do don't touch those cases. If you lay a hand on them you'll have every man in this dock out on strike, and what's more it'll be the last load you'll pick up here.'

'But do you mean to tell me that we all have to suffer the rudeness and stupidity of a blasted little official like that?'

'Yes I do. People like him rule the docks these days.'

'In that case I'm sorry for trade unionism. That bastard is subhuman. He's not a man. He's a walking, talking machine with a hat on.'

'Think what you like, but around here say and do nothing, you particularly.'

'Why me particularly?'

'Because it is out. Everybody knows you're a Number One. You, friend, represent "private enterprise". Follow?'

I didn't trouble to explain that I was not a Number One. They would not have believed the truth if I had told it. So all I did was to walk slowly back to the boats, thinking about the sadness of it all and wishing the day had not been spoilt by bitterness.

'You really must control your Irish temper, Jimmy. Come on. I'll give you a hand to stack these few, and we'll sheet-up. John, come on, sheeting-up.'

A head of light curly hair came up out of the engine-room. 'Coming, Missis.' John followed, his hands black, for he spent hours cleaning and checking, clearing the bilge pump, emptying the mud box, nursing his beloved engine. The day he had joined us I had taken him into the engine-room and said, 'What do you think of that?'

'Not bad, Captain. That's not bad.' He always called me Captain, and Gay Missis. 'In fact that is near as good as my father's.'

'Well I want you to keep her like that—always. If she blows anywhere, or splits a pipe, we shall be able to spot it immediately. Watch the oil levels, and put the tools back in the right place. Understand?'

'Yes, Captain. I like to see 'em like that.'

A few days later I was back in the engine-room to make sure all was well. She looked beautiful, but the little devil had already cut out the governor. I called him in.

'What have you done to this engine?' I spoke gruffly.

'Nothing, Captain, nothing.' The poor kid looked terrified. I spoke more quietly; repeated the question.

'I only unshipped the guv'nor.'

'Why didn't you say so in the first place?'

'Didn't think you'd notice, Captain.' He smiled.

'I probably know more about that engine than you do, boy, and don't forget it. What's the idea of cutting it out?'

He went into a long story all about governors, and it was interesting—so interesting that I decided to leave it as it was.

'All right. Now just two things. Don't ever alter anything else on these boats without asking first, and never tell lies.'

'Yes, Captain. I'll put it back proper.'

'Leave it as it is. We'll try her out this way. Might get along a bit faster, eh?' I patted him on the shoulder, and from looking miserable he relaxed into a smile.

Now, as he came towards us, I glanced at him and realized how different he was already from the shy, over-dressed young man who had first visited our boats.

'It's no good, Gay. Forget it. Go back to your sunbathing. We mustn't touch them, or, so I am told, we'll have the whole dock on strike. Don't worry, John. The loading isn't finished.'

'But that's bloody stupid! Can't we even help them?'

'No.' I told her of the office conversation. She let fly a whole string of oaths, and ranted on about trade unions and petty practices until I asked, 'Now who wants to learn to control her temper?'

John had listened to all this, and, as soon as his chance came, he cried, 'I heard what that man said to you, and what you said. Did you catch him? Did you shove him in the cut?' He looked excited.

'No, John, I didn't.'

'Oh that's a pity. He was a proper bastard.'

* * * *

They took just over five hours to stow 660 small cases into the boats, and we left Brentford without seeing our bowler-hatted friend again. Conditions were grand for boating. It was warm. The fields were green. The leaves, fresh and young, rustled on the trees. The engine sounded crisp, and the mate, up for'ard there, sang and jumped about on his counter, as if steering a seventy-foot boat was just a kid's game.

Gay was 'at home' in the cabin, making sandwiches and brewing tea. The radio was alive, playing records, and, as we rippled across the long pound from Norwood towards Cowley, Louis Armstrong came too. Blowing his horn as no other man can, gravel-voiced Louis sifted 'Gully Low Blues' through his vocal chords. Lil Hardin sang 'That's When I'll Come Back To You', and Billy Kyle, hands gliding, hands whipping, across the keys, fingers darting up and down, gave us 'Perdito' and 'Stompin' at the Savoy'. Lovely sounds! Satchmo with Lillian, with Earl Hines, with Billy Kyle—making real jazz.

All was fine with the world. A new trip was beginning, much of it on unknown waters, for our destination was Blaby, and we had never worked the cut to Leicester. The log rested on the cabin top. I opened it and wrote:

May 3, '49	13.00 hrs.	Leave Brentford
	15.15 hrs.	Bull's Bridge

The meal was ready. I stepped on to the gun'ale, then the cabin roof, and Gay passed up a full plate and a steaming mug. One in each hand I walked the length of the cabins and on to the top planks, now neatly covered by the sheets and crossed every three feet by taut rope. Along this ten-inch cat-walk to the fore-end deck I went, but I didn't have to call. That boy could smell food! Though I was twenty-five yards behind him even now, he had spotted my arrival. Down went the revs. The monkey slowed. The tow-line dipped, and, as the butty caught up, I drew the great rope inboard. Gay steered us alongside. Over to John went the food. The revs. jumped. He went ahead. I paid out the snubber. Gently he took the strain, and we were on our way once more.

That's how life could be, but seldom was, for long pounds are few and far apart. 'Fats' was playing 'Don't Let It Bother You' as Cowley Lock came into sight. A pair were in the lock heading up country, which meant work. I turned off the radio, and checked that everything was shut, and all stowed, all safe. 'Good-bye kettle.' I grabbed a bicycle from the back end of the hold, and was ready to jump. Over I went. Now Gay was at the helm. She brought her boat neatly alongside the monkey judged the moment to leave the tiller, and dashed along that great length of ten-inch plank to the bows. She was away now. John put his tiller over slightly, nursing the boats together as they moved forwards. Gay flicked a rope neatly over the stud on John's bows, made it fast to her boat and ambled aft, her work for the moment done.

Now John controlled both boats. They were breasted as they crept towards the lock. I had got there already. The lock-keeper was helping. Paddles were up and fifty to sixty thousand gallons crashed, swirled and careered down the cut towards our boats. The boats were held against the flood, glided through it, the steerer judging speed and time. The keeper and I each leant against a balance beam. Patience and pressure were needed. It was quite useless to push. One must bide one's time. Of a sudden they began to move, and as they did the revolutions of the monkey boat rose. The pair eased gently into the great wet chamber, which, now that one had become accustomed to it smelt sweetly of progress.

The boats were left in gear, with the prop. ticking over, so that all the time they were pressing gently forwards. Now we were all working, each on an agreed task. The gates were closed and top paddles raised, gently at first so that the incoming falls did not crash on to the bows; then more quickly. We watched them rise from the shadows into sunshine, and watched that the for'ard fenders did not foul the massive timbers of the gates. The din of falling water faded as the lock filled. Great eddies chased and played about the rising boats, and as the cabin-top came level with the parapet, Gay stepped aboard with the can she had filled from the lock-side water-tap. She undid her breasting straps, popped into the cabin and stoked the range or stirred a stew simmering on the shining top of the stove; then, with practised timing, walked to an upper gate, leant against a balance beam, and chatted a moment with John, who was leaning on the other.

They moved the gates, his first. It was open. He doubled back to his counter, which was already coming ahead. As he passed from the lock he leant over, reached the snatcher from the butty's bows and dropped it into the hook. Then he snapped his throttle shut, and watched the short tow-line take up—short now because we were at the foot of that great climb of many locks which would end at Cowroast. Gay was aboard. Into the rudder post went her tiller. Sweetly judged, the snatcher took the strain. The butty heeled a little and quickened, and both boats were away towards Uxbridge.

As soon as the paddles were raised, and it became a matter of waiting for the lock to fill, I had jumped on to Gay's small bicycle, charged along the towpath to the next lock, and begun the work of setting it fair for the oncoming boats. So onwards until the happy time when another pair were seen coming towards us, or I met an oncoming lock-wheeler. Then we stopped our crazy charging along the pitted path and had a yarn, and maybe a cigarette, and gave one another glad tidings of a good road. Finally I cycled slowly to the next bridge hole, waited, and, as the butty passed, jumped aboard, bicycle in one hand, the other ready to grip something firm and strong.

Now it was just a matter of filling locks, with three pairs of hands to do the jobs. John enjoyed the fun, passing on tips, cautioning us on any careless or silly move. That boy knew the faults or peculiarities of every lock on the canals we worked. 'Black Jack is a booger,' or 'Stockers is 'ard,' he would say, and once, when I was aboard with him, he turned to me and said, 'Mind yer 'ead. The next bridge is a tunnel.'

We made 'Ricky' that night, working until just before 8 p.m., and tied up above the lock after seven hours' boating. We had travelled eighteen miles and worked nineteen locks at an average of 2·5 m.p.h. On a road of that kind this was good going.

Absent-mindedly I had taken the tiller out of the rudder when we stopped, and, as in locks, rested it on the cabin top. The first tasks for John and me, as soon as the boats were secure, was washing them down, clearing and coiling straps, and examining the engine. Gay went down to prepare the food.

'Captain, may I tell you something?'

'Yes, of course.' He looked worried. I wondered what troubled him.

'We're finished for the day, and look at your tiller.' I looked. He went aft and knocked on the side of the cabin. Gay called, 'Come in,' as always, meaning 'Come aboard'.

' 'Tis only me, Missis.'

'Come on, John. Come aboard.'

He stepped into the steering well, raised the long curved tiller, turned it so that the curve inclined upwards, thrust it into the rudder post, and returned to where I was working.

'Does that matter so much?' I asked him.

'Oh yes. We've got to tell them we've finished. The tiller up like that in the rudder means we've packed in.'

Thus, little by little, I learnt from our seventeen-year-old teacher the customs, manners, habits and superstitions of true boaters. John's family never knew when they had come 'off the land', and his name was one recorded a hundred and fifty years back in the history of the waterways. His was a proud family, and he the product of all that was best, most enduring and most sad also about these little-known people.

In the engine-room we primed the diesel, wiped her dry and checked oil levels. Then together we moved into the butty well, and sat, one on either gun'ale, for our evening yarn, when we discussed the day, possible improvements in our boating technique, tomorrow's 'road', the cut, boating and boaters in general. I shall never forget those evening talks with young John. When the cut and boating were concerned he was the master, though less than half our ages. When we dealt with more general topics or any activities 'on the land', as he called it, his views were those of a child half his age, and a very strange child at that.

He spoke seriously of 'bad places', where 'bad people' attacked boaters and caused terrible things to befall them. Such places must never be passed after sundown; never should one tie up there for the night. At first I thought he must mean that it was difficult to moor there—that the banks were slippery or the water shallow, or that thugs played hell around. No, oh no, he didn't mean that. They were places where spirits, ghosties, moved about, and enjoyed pushing folks into the cut, undoing mooring lines and fooling around with engines so that they would not start.

'But, John, you don't believe in these ghosts? Not seriously?'

'That I do, Captain. We all does, and I wouldn't stay there or pass after dark. You mind what I'm telling you. It's true, and my father heard tell of a woman thrown into Stoke Bottom one night. They heard her scream once, no more. They got her out. She wasn't drownded, not even hurt, but she never spoke again. Just lied in the butty and died, she did.'

I looked at him as he spoke, and saw immediately his complete seriousness and credence. Never again did I laugh at his beliefs or try to dissuade him from them. But once more I was struck by the feeling that we were living in two eras. Months back at Hampstead Road top lock, I had felt this about the canal and our life upon it. Now, with John here, talking so seriously of his superstitions, I again understood that we moved in two widely-separated ages.

Combing her hair, Gay came up from the cabin and said, 'Grub will be ready in a few minutes. Hungry, John?'

'Oah yes, Missis. I like me rations.'

'Isn't it a perfect evening, and lovely to be sitting here warm and tired after a good day?' I said to her.

'Yes, it's all right now. My God, do you remember how we used to feel in the evenings? I shall never forget those early days and the cold during our ice age.' She ran her fingers across the comb, leaned from the butty and dropped the hair into the cut. Young John shot to his feet, and almost dived head-first into the water. With one hand clinging, he reached with the other, and grabbed the little heap of hair floating on the water. He picked it out, crossed the well, stepped on to the land and tucked the hair into the lower branches of a hedge. Then he came back and said, 'You didn't orter do that, Missis, or you'll go bald'.

'Don't be daft, John. What are you talking about?'

He looked at her, no smile on his face, and announced, 'If you throw your hair into the cut, you'll go bald, sure enough. It's like bandages. My ma told me long ago when I threw one in. "Now you've done it, boy," she said. "You'll never heal. Mark my words." And it didn't for ages. Got worse it did, bigger and bigger.'

'And eventually?' I asked.

'Oh, come the end it did, but she was right, and I never done it again.'

'What awful rubbish . . . ' Gay began. I touched her ankle with my foot, looked at her and just shook my head. 'Come on,' I said. 'How's the supper? I'm faint.'

We all went below and started some other topic, but I was thinking about John's mother and her wise if strange form of teaching. She was bringing up her children to respect the canal, to keep from it all the rubbish which landlubbers contribute. They must never throw anything in which might one day foul a boat's propeller—no bandages, no ropes, no sacks, tyres, wire, not even the hair from a comb. Her method was the powerful one of inculcating superstitious fears, as, no doubt, her mother had done. And children of the cut were also told of 'bad places', places dangerous for them to play around, and 'bad people', who would push you into locks if you were stupid enough to walk by the edges in the dark.

Obviously we had much to learn if we were not to seem a stupid couple to John. Above all, I wanted not to hurt his feelings, and so I asked him to point out our mistakes and to teach us the customs and manners of his people. He was delighted at the request, and I think that thenceforth he considered there was some hope of making boaters of us. On our part we were fascinated and interested by the innumerable things he told us.

* * * *

The sky was brilliant the following morning, but a full gale was blowing. We had, of course, experienced the effects of wind before, but certainly nothing quite like this. In the longer pounds, loaded as we were, we had to bear up all the time. The road was bad, Gay was lock-wheeling because she didn't like steering under these conditions, and, as I worked away at the tiller, I didn't blame her. We had passed Lot Mead and were heading towards Croxley Green when it happened. Gay jumped on her bicycle, and was charging along flicking the handlebars to miss the larger pot-holes when a great gust hit her broadside on. She was, as usual, wearing trousers. Above them were two or three woollies, covered over all by a red waterproof ski-ing jacket with the hood up. Her broadside was quite broad. She didn't hesitate. In fact from our vantage points, although we guessed what had happened, it really looked as if she did it on purpose. She just rode straight over the edge and into the cut.

For a moment only a bicycle wheel and two blue-clad legs were to be seen—a peculiar V-sign from the water. There was nothing that we could do to help, so we thoroughly enjoyed the sight. She got right way up after a short time, and climbed out lugging the bike behind her—both black and encrusted with the peculiarly pungent-smelling mud of the cut. I was pleased to see that she was laughing and soon ducking first the bicycle and then her lower self, in an effort to remove the filth. At Croxley she came aboard, and John and I worked two-handed through the next pair of locks, while she changed and washed her clothes. For the rest of the day we boated along with her assorted attire flapping like mad from the strings which held our top sheets in position.

'Are you taking over or going lock-wheeling?'

'Booger that for a lark! You have a go, and I hope you fall in an empty lock, funny guy. I saw you laughing. Just you wait till John sees his supper tonight. He was so creased with laughter that he nearly fell off his counter. I'll teach him! Go on. Hop it. I'll steer.'

Through Kings Langley and Berkhamsted we had a bit of luck, as two pairs came down leaving us a few open locks. On one was a young girl, and the sight of her unbalanced our mate, which really didn't surprise me. She was, I suppose, about John's age, slim, with a boy's figure, no curves, but a beautiful face and neat, shapely legs. Her head was covered with the usual coloured square. Her skin was dark as if deeply sun-tanned, cheek bones high and eyes bright, smiling, alert. She wore a rather short printed cotton dress. As she worked around the lock plenty of her pretty legs was visible for all to admire. As she passed the monkey boat, a deal of banter flew between her and John. Passing Gay she called the usual 'How d'you do?' and smiled.

As our pairs separated, I watched the mate waving, and, to my amazement, turning swift somersaults over and under the metal tiller of his boat, and steering at the same time. I wondered if this was some significant sexual exhibition of young boaters or merely normal juvenile showing off. I made a mental note to discuss the performance with him.

Cowroast at last! To John's disgust we insisted on our now habitual breather, during which he discussed brass and brasses with me. It appeared that it was rather degrading for him to be mate on a pair which did not have three brass bands around each 'chimley' nor a loop of 1- or 1½-inch brass in the top of the engine exhaust stack. To do the job 'proper' we should also have three brass 'balls' one above the other just inside the cabin door, on the left, above the range. It took me a long time to discover that these 'balls' were knobs of old bedsteads.

Steerer Phelps told me later that there was no reason for this. It was only a matter of tradition and decoration. Eventually we had our brass balls, and forever after I was delighted by them. They were polished every day; and at night, when the cabin lights were on, each reflected a curved picture of the interior. They were quite charming.

We arrived at the bottom of the Marsworth Flight at 3 p.m. Gay and I decided that another evening in the 'Red Lion' would be a great idea, as we had not stopped there since our January visit. To John's surprise and disgust I gave orders to tie up.

'What *now*, Captain?'

I explained that we had friends in the pub.

'But we've only just started.'

Some boy this! We had, according to the log, crept from our beds at 4 a.m., cast off from Ricky at 5.55 a.m., boated for 8 hours 50 minutes, travelled 21 miles and worked forty-three locks!

To console him, I passed over a ten-shilling note and said, 'You go into the town, and see if you can buy some brass strip and balls. Don't spend all that, mind. I want some change.' He beamed, and disappeared into his cabin. Later, while Gay and I were washing and making ourselves beautiful, we heard his cabin doors slam and the padlock click on them. Then came a knock on our cabin wall.

'Hullo, what do you want?'

'Can I borrow Missis's bike, Captain?'

'Yes, go ahead. The lamps are in the engine-room. Don't bust it up.'

'Bye then, Captain. Bye, Missis. I'll find that brass somewhere.'

'He's a nice kid,' Gay said.

'Amazing, I think. Do you know he reckons we're soft? Don't work long enough hours? He was quite peeved about us stopping here.'

'No wonder the lad is so skinny. Seventeen only, works like mad and has really very little sleep. You don't think we're overworking him, do you?'

'*We*, good God! He's overworking *us*. Whatever are you worrying about?'

'My seams. Are my seams straight?'

Turning from my shaving mirror, I suddenly saw a vision in the far end of the cabin. Gay stood looking over her shoulder at her legs, which were clad in dark nylons.

'Are they straight, dope? What are you looking so startled about?'

'What's on? Are you going to a dance or something?'

'Look, I've worked like a black today and been blown into the black cut. Now I'm going out in a nice black dress just to make a change. Any complaints?'

'I should say not.'

'You get cleaned up, and put on a respectable pair of bags for a change. Are you going to wear a shirt?'

'No!'

'All right. Don't shout. At least you might wear a clean jersey.'

It certainly made a pleasant change to feel clean and comparatively smart, but I had no regrets for the life I had left. Relatives and acquaintances smugly accused me of 'escapism', and spoke as if, by leaving the herd, and what they even called 'the rat race', I had sinned against humanity and myself. Some were outraged, some jealous; I don't think any understood.

To me, this leaving of a useless life and a habitual round of boring pastimes was like going into the desert to think, to recover some manliness, regain some self-respect. The escape was from them only. I had taken myself with me, as every man does everywhere. Already, sitting outside and looking inwards at myself, I knew I was healing. This life in the open places, so close to the earth, the seasons, the creatures of earth and air, was already tuning up my senses. I was thinking more clearly, not just how to get round that bend, but about things which really matter. My feelings were already wider, deeper. The mildew was off them. I was seeing, hearing again, and appreciating sights and sounds—the flashing kingfisher, the dawn chorus, young lambs leaping, the sweet song of soaring skylarks. All these I had come to love as a child. I had lost them for years in London, found them again on hills and in fields during the war, and lost them anew since the war's end and my enforced return to office and factory life.

My body then was soft, a flabby heavy case for the five senses. Now it was back in trim. My neck with its three damaged bones was doing well. At least it didn't ache, though every time I jumped aboard from lock sides I felt a jar. My left arm, useless a few years before, was now doing a fair job. If over-strained it protested, but, considering its past condition, I was pleased. Remembering the old doctor at Roehampton, I couldn't withhold a smile. 'You're finished for anything tough, you know. Those bullets have done irreparable harm. I don't want to make an invalid of you, but always be careful. Don't fall or lift things. Don't jar yourself in any way. As for your arm, I'm afraid you will have to consider yourself one-handed. The other hand is not, quite frankly, likely to regain much strength. Have a care now.' I wished he would come boating with us for a day. He would see just how wrong he had been.

I thought of the past as I stood there in the 'Red Lion', a pint in one hand and the other resting on the bar. I felt that the decision to quit London and move on to the cut was one of the best decisions of my life.

As always, we had a convivial evening in the pub, and returned to the boats much later than we had intended. John was not back yet, and I wondered whatever the boy could be doing at this time of night.

We were awakened by a loud hammering on the cabin side. I sat up, and called out, 'Hullo. What's the matter?'

'It's five, Captain. Thought you'd like to know.'

'Thanks, John. Couldn't have heard the clock.'

We had overslept by a whole hour, and our taskmaster was displeased.

At about 7 a.m. we cast off, and began what turned out to be one of our finest days of boating. The wind was gone. The sun shone brilliantly. Everything went well. There were no accidents, no mistakes and a fair road. All of us seemed brighter after our little bit of laziness the previous day, and the mate walked up, down and around his counter, turned innumerable somersaults, and sang for hours so loudly that we, though far behind, could clearly hear. Through the locks we charged, concentrated on our tasks. We took the hellish Blisworth Tunnel flat out. At the top of Stoke John opened the throttle wide, and cracked into the darkness. I watched him disappear into the hole and was fascinated to see ahead only the shortening brown snubber—a kind of umbilical cord joining us to nothing visible. Then in we went, and away ahead heard the echoing din of the exhaust, note unchanged, going like the hammers of hell.

That young devil meant us to learn the hard way. There was no doubt about it. As always I got the wobbles, began tacking and striking the wall, but he didn't let up for a second.

At 7.30 p.m. we tied up at Gayton, by the junction with the Northampton Arm, and my log showed that we had boated for 12 hours 20 minutes, travelled 37 miles and worked 25 locks. It was an average of three miles an hour, and on a road of that kind this was real boating by anybody's standards. Our duties to the boats all done, we sat for a gossip, Gay and John on the cabin tops, myself in the steering well of the butty.

'I'm worn out. This is no life for a woman. I can feel all my muscles aching, and before I didn't know I had any.'

'It was a great day though. Averaged three, John. How's that?'

'Not bad.' He smiled. Obviously no bouquets were coming from him.

'I got the brass. I'll fix it at Blaby.'

'Good lad! Any change for me?'

He reached into his pocket and handed me back the ten-shilling note.

'I only gave you ten bob. How come?'

'That's all right. I found it.' Again he smiled.

'What have you been up to, young John? Where did you "find it" as you say?' Gay looked towards him. 'Come on. Tell us.'

'That don't matter. I got around yesterday—Tring, Aylesbury and back down the cut. I found her.'

'Who's "her"? Come on. You've a saucy look in your eye.' Gay was interested.

'The girl we met yesterday. She and me was courting way back, but me mum stopped it. She's Emma Buck. She was scared of my mum, but now I'm with you it's all right again.'

'She's a very pretty girl,' I said, and, somewhat nervously, for I didn't want to lose our mate, asked, 'Are you going to marry her?'

'No, but we're courting again, Emma and me. She's going to write to me at Leicester.'

'Oh good. She can write then?'

'No, not she, but she'll find someone as can. I want to write E and B, Captain. You'll show me how, won't you?'

'Of course, John. Would you like me to teach you to read and write?'

'That I would. If I could read and write I could go on the land and get a proper job like some of me mates. The Army teached they, and they never come back.'

'But,' said Gay, 'you love the cut. What would you do on the land? You'd be unhappy, John.'

He looked at her, this seventeen-years child, and replied, 'It's the women. They all want to leave the cut. Them as *has* gone talks to the women about cinemas, dancing and all what goes on. All the women wants to leave the boats.'

I sat there thinking about the absurdity of the Government's decision to force all the young men from the cut into National Service, from which few returned. During the war the canals played an invaluable part in transport. Every effort was made to find crews for pairs. Along came girls and women. The canals were vital. Now, by forcing the young men into the Services, the nation had lost a generation of boaters. The boys on leave rushed back to their boats, and spread the news of the wonders ashore. They painted a world unknown to their younger brothers and sisters, and told only of its pleasures and excitements. The daily grind, slums, queues of automata at factory clocks, huddled heaps of homeless people — these were never seen.

The boys from the cut were taught to read and write, to drive lorries, to clean their teeth, to become dissatisfied with their life on the canal. But after their discharge from the Services, what?

An unskilled job, a street corner, a cheap dance-hall floor, a steamed-up 'caff' to spend their evenings in, a sordid room in a dirty lodging house to return to at night. This, in their innocence, they would take instead of life on the cut. I felt deeply for them, and could appreciate their reaction as the novelty wore off and the realization of their tragic mistake dawned.

Already I had discovered, as others had before me, that the continued existence of these true people of the cut, this hard core of descendants of the original navigators or navvies who dug the 'roads' and puddled the clay of the pounds, was an anachronism. Not only had so-called 'progress' passed them by, but their environment and way of life had deeply marked and sharply moulded their unsophisticated natures and given them —I mean this in the most worthy sense—childlike characteristics.

Certainly some were dirty. Of course a few battled outside pubs at closing time. Most could neither read nor write. There was hardly a mother among them who had not, because of her physical exertions, had two, three, or even more miscarriages. But the children who were born, seen sitting, maybe, on their naked bottoms on a concrete hard, were strong, tough and beautiful. Hill's boy at nine years of age steered his father's boat and felt king of the world.

'But,' say the do-gooders, 'they cannot even read.' No, maybe not, but, if they could, what would they read? The lowest products of the Press, the trashy sex and violence of the bookstalls which draw little crowds to their windows, advertisements which persuade and encourage them to spend more than they earn. 'But,' the do-gooders reply, 'some might learn to appreciate good books; might educate themselves even.' Agreed, some might, and then what? They would gradually appreciate that they were trapped in a herd, exerting all their energies, spending their precious short lives, to keep up in the rat race. Then, with the shock of violence, they would understand that the old life, that dearly, fondly-remembered life, held more possibilities for true happiness than the one they were now suffering.

We asked the elderly boaters, 'Where were you born?' Nearly always the answer was the same—'On a boat'. 'Do you long to go on the land?' 'No, never.' 'Do you want to die on your boats?' 'We was born on 'em, and lives all our lives on them. Where else would we want to die?' 'What do you like about the life on the cut?' 'Being on the move, our homes with us. The countryside. Music and singing in pubs of an evening.'

We were invited into their homes, and marvelled at the order and contents of the small cabins. Ranges and chimneys were not just polished but glistening, reflecting the complete cabin. There was lace everywhere, on shelves, hanging pinned to woodwork. Hand-painted china plates had china lacework rims. Brass rails and brass knobs unscrewed from old bedsteads were fixed firmly to the cabin timbers, and ornate vases were filled with flowers from the hedgerows.

Like children they love colour and toys. If they trust you, they find satisfaction in showing you the simple things which give them pleasure. They are a truly happy people, kind and simple, a little-known race existing apart, asking nothing but work and a small and completely inadequate payment, but above all to be left alone to lead their lives as they wish. They do not want to be saved or have their conditions improved by people on the land. These people scorn them, and are so unmannerly as to poke their faces into their homes, while they, when passing boats, avert their eyes in customary respect for another's privacy.

They *are* saved. They *are* educated. They long ago learned a simple philosophy: 'Give us peace in our work, friendliness in our clan. Let us have the fields and skies about us, the fresh air, be it cold or warm. Let us watch the colours of the seasons, and enjoy their sounds and smells too. Let us enjoy our simple pleasures—our castles and roses, our brass, our painted cans. Leave us to live and work on the cut, and die in our boats which we love. That is all.'

'Hi, you, where have you gone to?' Gay's voice broke my thoughts and brought me back. Thank God I was still there.

'Sorry, I was thinking. Where were we? Oh you wanted me to teach you to read, John.'

'And write, Captain. I know some. I know my nishils. I'm J R and she's E B.'

'All right. I'll teach you in the evenings. We'll buy some simple books with this ten shillings, but you must promise me something.'

'What's that then?'

'You must listen to me and believe what I tell you just as I do you. I shall teach you other things than reading, things I want you to understand.'

'I will. Oh yes, I will. When shall us start?'

'Tomorrow. Now tell us about our road on from here.'

He began his description of the Leicester Arm, and the longer he talked the more terrified I became. It sounded a horror, just a mass of tunnels, single locks and bow-hauling. Gay was below preparing food. We heard her call, 'Get some water you two. I'm nearly out.'

Still yarning we walked with the cans to a beautiful brass tap. There it was—handsome, easy to see, well placed. I hung the handle of the first can over it and turned on. Nothing happened. It was beautiful but useless.

So it was that John and I became both pupil and teacher—rôles which were to last, to the advantage of each of us, until the sad and bitter ending. And because of these memories—the start of our mate's education and the tap which had no water—I shall always recall Gayton Junction.

* * * *

May 6, '49	04.45 hrs.	Arise.
	07.00 hrs.	Leave Gayton.
	11.30 hrs.	Turn into Leicester Arm.
	20.20 hrs.	Moor Foxton Top Lock.

13 hrs. 20 mins. on move. 35 miles covered. 14 locks.
Average: 2·6 m.p.h.

Remarks: Cut starts with a swing bridge. One member must go ahead and open it. Leicester is 42 miles distant.

LOCKS. 1-7 are single, called Watford's. Takes 55 mins. to work. Bow-hauling.

N.B. Wind paddles down. Do not drop them. Reason—connecting link between paddles and lifting gear is made of wood.

After Watford's come 'Twenty Mile Pound' and Crick Tunnel, 1,528 yards, but straight and, according to John, ' 'aunted bad'. Cut twists, weedy. Channel muddy. Then comes Yelvertoft, and, on right, entrance to Welford Arm. Then another tunnel, which is easy—1,166 yards, Bosworth, then Foxton Top.

These are the bare bones of what was a most beautiful day of boating. We had the feeling all day that we were on top of the world and alone in it. Of course we passed a few buildings and saw a few people, mostly small distant figures, but generally the world was ours, shared only with water-fowl, game, cattle, sheep and birds. We could see for miles in all directions, and I discovered later that we were 400 feet above sea-level. To us it felt that we were on a small, winding, abandoned river rather than a canal, for the meadows were fringed on both hands by tall reeds. We meandered along the narrow channel between, frightening the life out of all the fowl and regarded with surprised disdain by brilliant pheasants and quiet, grey herons fishing along the margins.

All this was true and was delightful, but to me it was also saddening. We glided by crumbling wharves, were slowed and had to force a course through mud in many places. The intense sensation of being, and moving, where no other man passed suggested to me only one thing—that very soon, if action were not taken, this beautiful Leicester Cut would become impassable for loaded boats.

All day the sun shone, and a heat haze lay over the land. Ahead, the reeds and rushes, startled by our coming, seemed to waken and courteously bow at our approach. As we went by, they leant backwards. When we had passed they broke into animated conversation, which was like the sound of rustled taffeta. The haze, the rhythmic dancing of the rushes, the ceaseless unfolding of this winding strip of high-bordered cut began to charm my senses. I wanted to sleep, to dream of moving onwards like this, in warmth, in peace, in beauty, for ever. But quite suddenly it was all over. We arrived at the edge of the plateau, and there ahead was a small house perched, as it appeared from our boats, on the brink of a chasm.

We made fast and looked around. Below, as far as the eye could see, spread a great plain. Somewhere in the vastness was Leicester, and somehow we had to get there. Again came the feeling of unreality—as upon the aqueduct over the Ouse and our first passing through Blisworth Tunnel. Our boats, it seemed, must take to the air or we must stop, for it would be impossible to lower them into that far-off country. We walked ahead and discovered the solution—a staircase so steep and so narrow that it almost gave me vertigo to look down it.

Gay was in the cabin cooking the evening meal. I called to her. 'Come on out. Come and look at this. See where we are.'

'Be with you in a few minutes.'

John and I were mopping the boats when he said, 'Remains of old lift is over there, if you want to see it.'

Gay's head appeared. She came ashore and looked round. 'Booger me!' she exclaimed. 'Where on earth are we? Or are we in the sky? Oh my God! Do we go down those?'

'Yes. That's Foxton, and down we go in the morning.'

'Them's nothing, Missis. They're easy.'

'Listen to him! Why, its indecent really. You know, before we came on the cut, I thought they were more or less level. We do seem to get ourselves into the most extraordinary places.'

'It's a wonderful view though, isn't it? Dear old cut! Just one surprise after another. There's something almost unreal about it all. Come on. We're going for a stroll. Lead the way, John.'

'My cooking! Wait a minute. How long shall we be?'

'Just a few moments, Missis. It's only over there.' He pointed.

She was back shortly. 'Where are we going?'

'Do you remember reading in *Narrow Boat* about the inclined plane lift at Foxton?'

'No, I don't. What was it?'

I explained to her how the boats were encased in great tanks on wheels, and drawn on rails up an immense concrete slope. The tank ascending was balanced by one descending, and both were controlled by cables powered by a steam-driven winch.

'Why, that must have been worse than floating in mid-air in aqueducts, Jimmy.'

'I bet it was good,' John remarked.

All we found was ruins—the remains of the engine-house and a great concrete slide, cracked and broken, with bushes and trees growing through the fissures. But standing looking down these remains, which seemed not to belong there at all, one realized how great had been the achievements of the engineers, who pioneered so bravely and with such remarkable success. Foxton Plane was not one of the original feats of the great masters. It was built at the start of the twentieth century, but nevertheless it was the result of big, brave, original thinking, and to see it now, crumbled, soon to be engulfed, once more brought a feeling of sadness.

The solution of engineering problems by brilliant men like Brindley, Jessop, Rennie and Telford, in the creation of the inland waterways of England and Wales, must, in their age, have seemed almost miraculous. I could imagine the awe and wonderment with which the average man of those times must have looked at structures like Pont Cysyllte Aqueduct, and at cradled boats climbing a steep hill, or gliding into the bowels of the earth and coming out unscathed at the far end. But wondrous achievements of yesterday are today commonplace. Tomorrow they are forgotten and decay. Along the Leicester Arm this feeling came strongly, and I wondered for just how much longer this lovely cut could continue to fulfil its purpose.

That same evening I wrote an alphabet for John, relating each letter to a place or thing on the cut. Thus A was for aqueduct, B was for butty and 'Bawtry', C was for cut and 'Chiswick'. I used mostly short words he knew well, such as oil, Mafas, toll, lock and strap. Finally I gave him pencil and paper, and set him the task of copying the whole thing out. He climbed on to his cabin top, and didn't move until Gay called him for supper.

The following day we dropped down the Foxton locks, passed the Market Harborough Arm, shot through Saddington Tunnel and worked our way gently up the locks along the fourteen miles to the Ministry of Food depôt on the outskirts of Blaby. We tied up there at 2.30 p.m., having covered 124 miles in 48½ hours.

To our surprise, and annoyance, we found three pairs of boats waiting to be unloaded. Gay came back from reporting our arrival at the office. 'Comic guy in there says we may be here until next Friday. Today's only Saturday, so I can't make out what he's thinking about, if anything.'

'Damn me. It shouldn't take that long! There's a crane and a conveyor here. What's the hold-up?'

'He says they have only one lorry. It's filled here from the boats; then motors round to that large shed for unloading by the same gang.'

'One lorry only!'

'Yes, 24 to 28 tons unloaded a day. They work today and tomorrow, although it's a Sunday.'

'Oh well, that at least is something.'

Again the same problem. We work hard, we hurry, we arrive full of hope, and find inefficiency. Annoyed, I reached for the chopper, went ashore and cut kindling. Then I went into the back end and broke coal to fit into the small range. We de-sooted the range, and I removed and cleaned the chimney inside and polished it outside. I cleaned and oiled Gay's somewhat battered bicycle, and finally I cleaned and polished myself. We dressed up and went into Blaby for a beer, determined to drown our sorrows. But we failed even to do this. Blaby was dull and uninteresting, and the pubs were worse.

We slept and lazed until 11.30 on Sunday morning, and felt quite wicked about our laziness. Gay said, 'Ooh, but isn't it nice? I think I could do this every morning.' I had to pull her out of bed on to the floor.

During the remainder of the morning and the afternoon we scrubbed out, cleaned cupboards, dusted shelves and tidied drawers. By this time I felt so virtuous that I suggested evensong to Gay.

'What do you mean? Evensong? Where? What's come over you?'

'Evensong service, stupid. In Leicester Cathedral.'

'I didn't know Leicester had a cathedral. Is it nice?'

'I don't know. I've never been there.'

'Not the cathedral. The service. Don't be so dim!'

'Oh yes. Beautiful singing. I like it. Very uplifting.'

'Good, we'll go. I could do with some uplifting.'

We went to church, and immediately afterwards Gay said, 'Now I'll take you to *my* pub'.

There is a story behind this remark. Leicester has some large stores. In them, on numerous occasions, Gay had modelled beautiful and expensive clothing. The girls were booked into a most staid hotel, where it would be impossible for anything untoward to happen to them. It was dull in the extreme. The hotel shall remain nameless, and I must point out that some years had passed since her last visit. She wanted to return for old time's sake, to revive memories of how, in their exuberance, they had surprised and alarmed the ancient inhabitants of that establishment. Her suggestion therefore bored me, and I wondered if anything as coarse as a pint of good bitter would be obtainable. Still, I graciously condescended to suffer the visit.

We found our way into a most comfortable lounge, discreetly lit, carpeted and graced by a magnificent bar, again well lighted. There was no glare; just a golden sunshine on polished glasses and coloured bottles of every shape. Beer-engine handles, claret-coloured, chrome-topped, ranged the counter. Behind them stood or worked three beautiful girls. Or at least they looked beautiful from my vantage point. Gay said it was all make-up. I disagreed because I was not looking only at their faces. However, about these girls, one was a blonde (phoney, according to Gay), one a brunette, and the third a red-head (tinted, Gay said). The blonde's hair was short and curly, the brunette's was pitch black, with a fringe, page-boy I believe they call it—marvellous; but the red-head, by jingo what a sight! Her hair was aflame, middle parted, tumbling in curves and curls to her shoulders—exquisite! The blonde had a V-necked dress, the brunette's was U-shaped, the red-head's O-shaped, all three plunged far enough; the curves above their waists were outstanding, when they turned about and bent to draw bottles from racks, I noticed that those below were also adequate. Their dresses, other than at the neck, were identical: blue jersey wool with horizontal white lines across them at about two-inch spacing.

Grouped at each end of the counter were two or three more attractive girls, some sitting, some leaning backwards on bar stools, all smartly rigged but perhaps with a little too much ostentation. There seemed to be yards of legs everywhere, much of it above the knee; and a collection of high-heeled shoes, so high that one wondered if it was possible to do anything but stand still on them. These girls prattled like canaries, and ceaselessly looked around. If any man moved, either into or out of the bar, up to or away from the counter, they fixed their eyes on him, watched and smiled. Nothing escaped them. Whilst Gay made herself comfortable at a small table at the back of the room, they stared, and looked displeased, as if something foreign and not quite nice was moving there. A few men stood at the counter, in groups and singly. Others sat at tables reading evening papers or laughing and chatting quietly with women.

I walked to the counter, and eased in between a man reading a paper and a couple of pairs of attractive knees, wondering which of the three wonderful Hebes I would draw. The brunette stood before me. 'Good evening, sir. What can I do for you?'

I ordered our drinks, but, thinking aloud I suppose, added, 'By God, you're a lovely-looking girl!'

She smiled sweetly, curtseyed quite elegantly, thereby

presenting me with an even fuller view of her curves, and said, 'Thank you, sir'. To me and to the girls beside me she commented, 'What a man! He says what he thinks. Most only look.' A burst of laughter followed this, and one of them, looking straight at me, cracked, 'You can cut that out. Betty's on duty, whereas I'm not.'

'Ah,' I answered sadly, 'lucky girl. But the trouble is I'm on duty too.'

There followed another peal of feminine laughter, and, as I turned away with the drinks, she called, 'Bad luck, big boy. But there's always another day. Be seeing you.'

Back at the table Gay quipped, 'Having fun, big boy?'

'Oh shut up. Cheers.' I topped the pint, and it was excellent.

'So this is your "little pub"?'

'Yes, but, Jimmy, it's changed a lot. It was so dull. Now it seems quite gay.'

'Indeed. And this is where, in your youth and beauty, you and all the girls stayed.'

'Yes. I told you, didn't I?'

'I'm surprised at you,' I said very seriously, as if cross.

'Why? Don't you like the place?' She sounded quite hurt.

'Just watch points awhile, and you should guess why.'

We sat back and watched, and, with one exception in England, I had never seen anything quite so blatant. Rotterdam, Hamburg, Penang, Karachi—yes, they could match it, improve on it in fact, but this in England! I was amazed.

Every now and then a couple, arm in arm, drifted laughing, up the wide staircase. Others came down silently. Taxi-drivers incessantly arrived, had a whispered conversation, tossed back a quicky and left to be followed shortly by a cheery couple. Girls from the counter slid from stools and joined males at distant tables. Other girls came in and draped themselves carelessly on the vacant stools, or joined the gatherings at both ends of the bar.

Quiet but pleasant music wafted from unseen radios. Conversations were quiet in tone. Only laughter, the tinkling of ice on glass, the hammering of beer-engine handles, and the click of crown corks falling into metal containers broke into the even level of sound. But colour and movement abounded. Brilliant dresses swayed, jerked, flounced across the room, up and down the stairs. Hair of many hues waved across the chromatic background of lustrous bottles, and behind the counter those three beautiful barmaids crossed and re-crossed, bobbed up and down, wove a triple skein of colour. Everywhere were perfume and female flesh—faces, shoulders, legs and the swishing music of nylon and crisp materials. Whoever thought this lot up was something of an artist.

'Well?' I looked at Gay. 'What about it?'

'I think it's a nice place.'

I laughed.

'I do wish you would share the joke.' She sounded peeved.

'It's a whore-shop, stupid! Isn't it obvious to you? Haven't you seen what's going on?'

'Oh is it? Are all these girls tarts?'

'Quiet. Not so loud. They'd tear you apart!'

'A whore-shop. Well I'm blowed. I don't think I've ever been in one before!'

'I thought you and the girls always stayed here.'

'Oh don't be disgusting! I've told you it wasn't like this when we came.' She began pounding with her painful little fists on my leg.

'Hi, stop that you little devil.'

I must have spoken too loudly, for all the girls and a few of the men at the counter turned and looked at us. The men smiled. The girls looked outraged.

Gay was quite cross now. 'Be quiet or I shall go. You know perfectly well that we should never have been allowed to stay in a place like this. Come on. Let's get out of here if you don't like it.'

'Don't be silly, Gay. I was only pulling your leg. It's interesting though to think how much and how quickly places change.'

'Do you want to go?'

'Oh no. I'm very happy. In my element as you might say. Good beer, pleasant music, a bevy of beautiful girls—and you, of course.'

'Well get me another drink, Jimmy. Your mind is not on your beer, and you're taking ages.'

I went to the counter, drew the blonde that time, and had a friendly chat with her.

We had a few more drinks, and then it suddenly dawned on

me that we were talking a lot of rubbish, that all the girls looked like Angels, that Gay's eyes had an unusual sparkle and that I had begun to stutter—just a little.

'Shall we go home? I'm feeling tired, and you look a bit tiddly.'

Later, in the darkness of the cabin, with the old cut rippling away along our metal hull, she whispered into my ear, 'Jimmy?'

'Ah, what?'

'We must go to Leicester again sometime.'

'Rather. I'm all for it. We'll go tomorrow and the day after if we're still here.'

'Oh, that might be overdoing it, don't you think?'

'No, not a bit. It was excellent beer.'

'I don't know. Move over, I want some sleep.'

* * * *

On Monday at about 8.20 a.m. they started to unload the pair ahead of us. Two hours later the crane blew up, and all the gang swarmed round it making suggestions. An hour or so afterwards it began to work again. Meantime it had never occurred to anyone that the men could lift the cases out of the boats and load the lorry by hand. At noon a large vehicle drove into the depôt. The crane was stopped, and the whole gang moved away to unload this monster.

I went to the office, and complained about the whole performance. The clerk said, 'Hold on a minute. You're not the only boater here, and we've got other jobs besides worrying about you, mate.'

This riled me. I told him I was off to Leicester to report the whole stupid business to the Waterways Manager there. His attitude changed. He was unused to boaters who stood up for themselves. 'I'll see what I can do to hasten things,' he said.

We took a bus to the city, called on the manager, complained about the activities at the depôt and, I think, rather surprised that charming man. We were dolled up, Gay looking like a film star. It must have shaken him to think that we were 'boaters'! After this interview we both felt happier. At least we had done all we could to speed things up.

Then we went to look for books for John. We selected two good illustrated alphabet books, and the oddity of the reason for their purchase struck us forcibly. Again the feeling of unreality about the cut life swept over us.

We walked for miles, did a powerful amount of window-shopping, and then, feeling strangely exhausted, went to see the film of 'Hamlet', which was, we both agreed, one of the finest we had ever seen.

The evening was passed in 'Gay's pub', where we sat and talked about our life, life in general and the inevitable sadness of human existence. The pub was just the same as it had been the previous evening. Some of the men who came in had been there yesterday; so had many of the girls. The laughter, though it sounded a little forced, still rang out. We talked too seriously, went too far, too deep, and arrived at negative conclusions. At last I could stand it no more. I didn't want this healthy, worth-while life of ours to be spoilt by thoughts which led to despondency.

'Drink up, and let's cheer up. Enough of this. I refuse to accept it all. Let's have some wine, and escape the fears and sorrows and anger.' I looked at her. She smiled.

'Yes. Perhaps you are right. Get me a large one. I need it. It will bring me back to life.'

'That's the point. That is the great essential fact. We must go on living, feeling, thinking, trying to find a way beyond all this waste and triviality. I glimpse a consciousness of power and greatness within myself at moments. It came a few days ago in the Twenty Mile Pound—a mystical feeling of awareness. It comes when I hear some music. Do you know the feeling I mean?'

'Yes, I follow. Strange and different things bring it to me. It is overwhelming.'

'It is elusive, but one must catch at it, remember always that the potential is there. Otherwise I feel the mind must die, be killed. But the realization of this power within oneself makes life worth living. Hey ho. Large one did you say?'

'Yes—a whopper. I suddenly feel more cheerful.'

'Good. I'll get them. Then we can sit and study form; let the other self take over for a while.'

We returned to the boats feeling quite cheerful, but were cast down again to see that the pair ahead of us were still not unloaded.

On Tuesday, at intervals, they removed a few more cases from them. Halfway through Wednesday morning we were told to cast off, and proceed to the wharf in Leicester where we would be unloaded immediately! So passed four days at Blaby, in which time we could have reached the coalfields, loaded and started south on another trip. My feelings about it all were beyond expression.

It took us three-and-a-half hours to reach Leicester, and thirty minutes later a gang began to unload the butty. Both boats were empty by 5.30 on Thursday, but it had taken them more than twice as long to unload than to load.

We received 13s 6d a ton for this cargo, and carried 40½ tons, which brought us £27 6s 9d. But it was now ten days since we had left Brentford, and I worked out that on the basis of our present daily expenditure the cargo had been carried without profit. Now our only hope was a quick loading and return trip. Gay went to the office to report that we were empty, and asked for orders. In a few minutes she was back, out of breath and excited. 'You had better come over. The manager wants to know if you would like to go to Stanton in Derbyshire.'

'Derbyshire. Good God! That's in the North of England, isn't it?'

'I don't know where it is.'

'Derbyshire,' I repeated, and thought, 'Dales, hills which are nearly mountains. Never been into the county, but surely it's a hell of a long way from here.' Then an idea struck me. 'John, ever been to Stanton?'

'Yes, Captain. 'Tis over the Trent River and on up.'

'On up how far? How many days?'

'Oh, day and a half, I expect.'

'Many locks?'

' 'Tis not a bad road, Captain.'

CHAPTER VIII

Slag to London

I never could resist the chance to investigate the unknown, and the idea of taking our boats into Derbyshire appealed to me. We received orders, tanked up at the wharf, and were away early on Friday morning, with a trip card for slag to be delivered to Bristowe-Tarvia at Stockley—though I didn't know where that was.

With me, hope really does spring eternally. Gay has a more suspicious nature and is not fascinated, as I am, by unknown country. And so, as we headed north on a beautiful morning, she was quiet while I was excited.

For an hour all went well. Leicester was astern, Loughborough ahead, and the next lock was called *Birstall.* Just short of it the engine died on us as if in deference to the name. We dived for the engine-room. It reeked of diesel oil. There was a puddle of the stuff over the floor, and it was pouring from our main feed pipe which had split wide open.

We had the pipe off in minutes, and John was going, flat out, back to Leicester on Gay's bicycle even before I had finished swearing. Within two hours he had returned with a new length and we had bled the system of air, and were on our way again. We worked like demons that day, and tied up above the first lock after crossing the River Trent. The log showed 24 miles and 18 locks in just under eight hours.

It really was a most exciting road, and I feel sure that, if John had not been with us, we should never have found the way. Along much of it there was no longer any towpath. Rivers came in on one side, crossed the pounds and crashed over weirs on the other. The locks all varied. Sometimes we needed small and large windlasses on one lock. In two locks we had to remove the fenders and fold the butty's rudder hard over in order to get the gates shut. We took umbrage at Loughborough for allowing a large factory to poke two pipes, high up its wall, about seven feet across the cut. The factory then squirted hot water from them, and this poured all over our boats and very nearly all over us. But at the critical moment I abandoned my tiller and dived into the cabin.

From Loughborough, through Bishop's Meadow and Radcliffe to Red Hill was all downhill work, and shortly after leaving Red Hill we boated on to what, to us, seemed a vast river. Opposite, quite far off, was Trent Lock. Beneath us was the deep water of Trent River, and the boats, freed of drag, shot ahead at a tremendous pace, going far faster than I should have thought possible. We fled across that river as if pursued or frightened to be boating in wide waters.

We were up at five next morning, and began the day of days. As usual we went flat out, through Long Eaton, past the junction at Sandiacre with the Derby Canal, through five locks and then, the engine at a tick-over, we worked the pair backwards into a cut over which a full-gauge railway track ran on an open metal bridge. This was a most odd and apparently insecure structure, from which hung lengths of rope—a baffling form of decoration.

'Office is up there.' John pointed. We looked and saw, not a factory, but a whole town of vast buildings and great, high, belching chimneys. It was a works without visible boundaries, the famous Stanton Ironworks. I knew the name well enough for, like any motorist, I had for years been passing great dumps of circular black pipes stacked along roadsides, and on each, in white, was written STANTON.

Gay jumped for the bank and called, 'I'll have a go at them, but I've just realized it's Saturday. I'll bet we're here until Monday at least.'

'Oh God, I'd forgotten! See what you can do anyway. It's only 10.15. They might load us this morning.'

'Some hope!' she called over her shoulder.

John and I made the boats fast. Then, as I reached for the mop, he said, 'Shouldn't worry, Captain. It will be a waste of time.'

'Why's that?'

He laughed. 'Wait till you've been loaded with slag. You'll know.'

Gay was missing for about an hour, but eventually appeared

swinging the bus-conductor's leather bag which she used as purse and handbag, and smiling all over her face.

'Any luck?'

'Yes, this afternoon, immediately after lunch, about one o'clock. What a place, Jimmy. I've been nearly all over it, met lots of people, had tea and biscuits twice, and seen all kinds of wonderful things.'

'How come?'

'Well it's a vast place, and I got lost; so I just popped into offices and asked. You should have seen their faces. I don't think most of them had ever seen a boater before, and, when I told them I'd come to have my boats loaded, they looked at me as if I was daft.'

'What happened then?'

'Oh they all said, "Sit down. Have a cup of tea. Have a biscuit. I'll ring up and find out. Hold on a minute," and so on. So I sat. It caused them an awful lot of trouble.'

'And eventually?'

'Well, I went from one office to another, past wonderful machinery, and finally to a very posh office where they have—what do you think?'

'I don't know. Go on. Come to the point.'

'They've got a boat-loading manager. Just think of that. Isn't it wonderful?'

'Pretty good. How did you get along with him?'

'Oh, he's sweet. He offered me a cup of tea and a biscuit, said, "Hold on a minute," and had a talk on the blower. Result—loading after lunch.'

'That's a bit of luck. Any idea how long it takes?'

'I forgot to ask.'

John, who had been listening to this story with his mouth open and a look of wonder on his face, chipped in, 'About two hours. They drops it in from trucks. We trim.'

'How do you mean?' I asked.

'Simple, Captain. See that bridge we came under. See them ropes. We goes under, holds the boat still, standing both ends and hanging on to the ropes. The truck's bottom opens, and the slag pours through the bridge into our holds. We trim by walking up and down holding on they ropes and moving the boats along. Some terrible dirty it is, I can tell you. Remember to shut your portholes and cabin doors, Missis. It's something horrible it is.'

Well, it might be horrible, but it seemed quick, which was our great concern. So we cleared our holds, had some food and waited. At one o'clock a very funny-looking engine came puffing along the line, pulling a string of V-shaped trucks. The first of these was halted above the cut, and we went into action on this strap-hanging lark under the bridge. It was horrible without a doubt. We all turned white and our boats also. Dust blew over everything, and like a low cloud it moved across the surrounding countryside. But in 1¾ hours we were full, trimmed, and, what is more, had 51½ tons aboard—risky perhaps but worth a try. The boats looked fine. The butty—slack boards in position, took her share. Loading lines were all in order. It was just a matter of depth of water between here and the main arm at Norton Junction.

That night we were back at Trent Lock, and it seemed to us almost impossible that we had travelled 12 miles, worked 10 locks and been loaded within a day. Such things just didn't happen on the cut; at least not in our sad experience. Good old Stanton Ironworks, we all agreed.

During lessons that evening I asked John, 'What is the idea of chalking JR over EB on the balance beams of all the locks we pass?'

'Because I'm courting. JR is me. EB is Emma Buck. That's right, isn't it?'

'Yes, and you're writing it quite neatly. But why?'

'I told you, Captain.' This quite impatiently.

'I'm sorry, John, but I don't follow. Don't see the point in scribbling on all the locks.'

'Well *we* does it. On the cut, always moving, we doesn't meet much, so when we're courting we tell her where we been. She'll come this way sometime and see it.'

'I follow. It's as if you were telling her that you were thinking about her.'

He looked quite shy at this suggestion, and replied, 'Yes, I s'pose so.'

'And does she do the same thing?'

'Oh no, leastways not yet.'

It was hard to pump information out of John, and he looked

at me, always, during these interrogations as if he were dealing with a very stupid person.

'You say, "Not yet". When does she begin writing then?'

'We might be courting some years. Then the time come when we got enough to get spliced, and we can have a pair. Then her people say it's right to go ahead, and sometime I'll see EB writ over JR, and I'll know.'

I set him a copying task after we had battled through some simple reading in his new books; then crossed to the butty and did my daily chore of polishing brass. John had been true to his word, and our three bands round the range chimney, and the bedstead knobs had been fitted while we waited at Blaby. At first he had suggested that I should clean them each morning but it was a messy game and I preferred to do it before washing in the evening. He was, I think, rather disgusted by my laziness. His were done first thing after we got under way each morning, and it amazed and amused us to see him keeping a straight course while he was running to and fro along his cabin roof polishing the ring round the top of the exhaust pipe.

* * * *

The journey went well considering our load and the state of the cut. Loughborough, we decided, was as bad a town as Leamington for people with dirty and stupid habits. There were those insulting pipes, and then we had the very devil of a job to get through the bridge-holes, and bumped over all manner of obstacles as we forced our way through the cluttered pound. However, on Sunday we averaged 2·3 m.p.h. over 24 miles, and on Monday 1·9 over 19 miles. This included 25 locks, and brought us to the foot of the Foxton Staircase.

It was a pleasant evening, but darkness came early, with the sky rolling up into great waves of thick cloud. The next day would see us back in Twenty Mile Pound, and we hoped for fine weather. But we awoke at 5 a.m. to the din of rain pelting on the cabin and a full gale buffeting the boats.

What a day that was! A battle from start to finish; with the Foxton locks early in the morning and the Watford Flight late in the evening. For the ten hours between, we stood gazing forwards, more or less still except for work with the tiller; and the wind-driven rain lashed us ceaselessly. It trickled down my skin and squelched in my shoes. Once we were truly soaked, the wetness didn't really matter except for the tickling of the trickles. But the cold became intense. All one's body warmth was washed away, and the wind evaporated the dampness.

Wednesday was better. There was much less wind, though it was still raining. It cleared during the evening, and we knocked back 35 miles, averaging 2·8 miles an hour, and tied up below Fenny's miniature lock, opposite the pub. Then we all agreed that we must go shopping. We changed from clothing which fell like wet bathing costumes on to the floor in a sodden heap. We wrung out our jerseys and trousers, stowed them in the cupboard in the back end of the steering well amongst wash-bowls, scrubbing-brushes and floor-cloths, and hoped that the sun would soon shine again. If not we should be short of covering.

John, for the first time, came with us into the pub. He drank ginger beer shandy, and chatted with all the other boaters there. We left him to enjoy the company of his people, but were amused and pleased to hear him referring to us frequently and telling them of our prowess. We were not conceited, but we were glad that the lad seemed happy with us, and, perhaps even more important, not ashamed to be boating with 'trainees'. We felt now that we were accepted by the boaters to a certain degree, for the shyness of their previous approach was gone, and the 'How d'you do?' expanded into conversations.

The sun returned to the cut next morning. Before we cast off, we brought the bow-hauling line out, and all our soggy clothes went aloft. Away we moved with a brave and colourful fluttering.

A Josher pair beat us to the start, and we were amused over a scene which concerned chickens. I had always thought these birds stupider than most creatures, but what occurred raised my estimation of them. All our boats have a small space right up for'ard, under the short fore-deck, covered with a hatch. Ours was used for stowing rope and spares of many kinds. Some boaters use it as a dog kennel; others have it fitted out as a tiny extra cabin. This Josher, and numerous other pairs, used it as a chicken-coop.

Well this boater, in a hurry to be away ahead of us, cast off, opened up wide and departed, leaving all his birds scratching away and enjoying themselves in the fields, after two days of enforced imprisonment during the bad weather. Eventually one old girl looked up, realized that they had all missed the boat, let out a frightful squawk, followed by a loud cackling, and beat it along the towpath. She was half running, half flying, head outstretched, beak open, uttering a flood of warning cries and aggrieved protestations.

All her friends immediately looked up, understood that they were now abandoned, and set off in noisy pursuit, one behind the other. There were seven or eight, all of various ages and agility, and the column gradually lengthened as they spaced and shrieked their way along. There was an extra cry when the saviour of them all was overtaken by a lightweight, rather attractive young thing, who had a flighty gait and absolutely no respect or concern for her elders.

As I watched, it suddenly struck me that these birds looked remarkably similar to some of the old women of the cut, who still wear voluminous skirts and black boots. When they run towards a lock they heave their hems high, lean forward and show their booted legs.

Now came the moment when these hens displayed unexpected intelligence. Each ran *past* the boat on which its coop was housed, stood on the edge of the path, watched its speed, checked its position; then, with a great thrust and flapping of wings, leapt screaming into the air and landed with beautiful timing on the deck. This alone showed considerable appreciation of the science of aim off, but even more remarkable for such creatures was the order in which they jumped. Instead of leaping in a stupid heap, as one might have expected, they took turns to make the awful flight. In fact one or two, spotting an early worm issuing from the earth, immediately ceased their cackling course and dallied, one eye on the queue and another on the grass, picking a morsel here and there before they took the leap.

Our day was hard, but the sun, the washed green of the trees and fields, and the recent memory of different conditions—all helped to keep us going strongly. We boated for just over twelve hours, along 26 miles, through no fewer than 41 locks, keeping up a 2·1 m.p.h. average on a really hard road. We moored at Fishery Inn.

'Oh, goody,' Gay exclaimed. 'A pub. Beer two nights running. That's the stuff. I can do with a few pints after today's efforts.'

'Well, John, how about that for a day's boating?' I asked, and for the very first time he smiled and replied, 'Oh, aye. It was a good day right enough, but we should never have let that Josher get ahead of us. We orter have catched him any road.'

I had forgotten this pair, and we had lost sight of them—which meant either that we had passed them without noticing, or that they had boated even faster than we. In these days, when things went so smoothly, and we worked hard and long, it seemed impossible to me that others could move more quickly. I suggested to John that we had passed them, and he laughed.

'No, I'd have seen them if they had tied up. Anyway I know they are just ahead of us.'

'How do you know that?'

'I heard them while we tied up. They're going on down.'

'You've got some hearing, boy. I didn't hear anything.'

'With engine off I can hear boats miles away and the paddles falling. I'm used to it, see. You'll maybe hear one day if you listen.'

'Time for lessons. Come on. I'll teach you something, you young blighter.'

He learnt fast, but his writing was terrible. He grasped the pencil in his thick, strong hand and gouged out words. I couldn't make him relax and ease the point up and down on the paper. His letters were tremendous in size, but he, like ourselves, was improving. Most striking was his ability to grasp simple figures, and at sums he went ahead at great speed. His keenness and excitement, as the understanding of pounds, shillings and pence came to him, was delightful.

We talked for a while during each session, or rather I talked and then invited him to ask questions. I tried hard to dissuade him from the notion that all young people 'on the land' were happier and better off than those on the cut. I savagely suppressed his romantic ideas, gained from the flowery reports of lads on leave from National Service, because I felt so strongly about the subject. I did my best to create a picture which toppled his dreams of 'caff', cinema, dance hall and street-corner society. I wanted to save him for his own happiness and for the good of the cut.

After a while he said, 'Emma writ me at Leicester'.

'Oh good, John. And someone read it for you?'

'Yes, a mate of mine at the wharf.'

'Have you answered Emma's letter?'

'No, Captain. That's what I wanted to ask you. Will you write to her for me?'

'Of course. But what if I write and then you copy it? Wouldn't she be excited to have a letter written by you?'

The proud young devil immediately replied, 'I mean to do that, but later when I can write proper'.

So began my courtship of Emma Buck, and I suppose that what eventually occurred was largely of my doing. Anyway, I like to think so, for I wrote that girl some, as John called them, 'smashing letters'. To begin with I asked him to tell me what he wanted to say, and he haltingly dictated the following:

Dear Emma,

I got yours in Leicester. I hope this finds you as it leaves me, well and at Fishery Inn with slag for Stockley. Top gate at Mountsorrel leaks awful, so we closed bottom gates. Our fuel pipe bust at Birstall, but I got it mended quick. Haven't seen my people. How's your mum and dad? Write to me at the Bridge.

Yours,

John Redknap.

I wrote it down, and then asked him if he would like me to make a few suggestions to brighten it up a bit.

'Oh yes, please, Captain. That would be smashing. You have a go too.'

We discussed my suggestions, and finally produced the following:

My dear Emma,

I was very happy and excited to find your letter waiting in Leicester. I hope this one catches up with you and finds you well and as beautiful as always.

We are moored at Fishery Inn because my Skipper likes to have a pint whenever possible. We have a load of slag from Stanton for delivery to Stockley.

On the way up to Derbyshire our main fuel pipe broke,

funnily enough at Birstall. But I rode fast on Missis's bicycle back to L., collected a new one and tore back to the boats before the Captain had finished swearing or clearing up the mess in the engine-room.

Remember me to your mum and dad and my people if you pass them. I haven't seen them for a long time, and have no idea what roads they have been on.

When you answer this letter, please address yours to the depôt at Bull's Bridge.

I hope we will soon meet again. Already it seems an age since our last meeting, but you are always in my thoughts.

'Bye, Emma my dear, and much love to you always.

Yours,

John Redknap.

I read it aloud to him.

'Cor, that's wonderful. That should keep her going for a bit. Reckon as how she'll be showing that to all the girls.'

'Do you want to put some kisses at the bottom?'

'Oh yes. I'll do that. You're good. I forgotten all about them. And shall us put "SWALK" on the envelope too?'

'O.K. As you wish.'

I handed him my pen, feeling very nervous about its survival. and said, 'Gently now. Tender kisses.' He covered the bottom of the sheet with crosses. I folded the letter, placed it in an envelope, stuck the flaps down and wrote, SWALK across the apex of the triangle. This, for the benefit of the uninitiated, stands for: 'Sealed With A Loving Kiss'.

As time passed, Emma found herself a worthy composer who, whether for fun or from a complete lack of inhibitions, wrote numerous quite startling letters to John. No punches were pulled, and sex reared a large though not ugly head. Dreams, daydreams, desires, imaginings—all were expressed in forthright terms.

These letters naturally led to discussions of sexual matters between John and me. He told me that, as far back as he could remember, he had known all about the physical relationship between his mum and dad. He had often heard and seen them playing around in their bed at the end of the cabin, while he was meant to be sleeping on the side bunk. They were covered at the start, and whispered so as not to wake him, but frequently he had either not been asleep or the rough and tumble had woken him up, and he listened to the giggles and creaking. Then, as the clothes fell away, he saw by moonlight, or the light of dawn brightening the cabin as it streamed through the thick round glass stud in the roof, his father mounted and the woman beneath him.

As soon as the children were old enough to be on their own, they were moved to the cabin on the other boat. But with men and women, boys and girls, living in such confined spaces, it was impossible for the children not quickly to become aware of their differences and to witness sexual play.

I asked him what experience he had had with girls. And, quite unlike lads of his age from towns and cities, he neither blushed with embarrassment nor boasted, but just calmly announced, 'I kissed a few, and squeezed them a bit. But I have never done anything much with a girl yet, nor likely to until I'm married—leastwise not a boater.'

'Why's that?' I asked, and he replied seriously.

'Because I'd get killed, and so would she. My dad and her dad would knock all shapes of hell out of me, and she'd cop it right and proper from her mum and dad.'

He used the common four-letter word, ' . . . ing about' and ' . . . ed a girl', without any gloating or smiling. To him it was a perfectly normal everyday word, like looking, or helping. Indeed he gave me the impression that, although he had, from such an early age, been fully aware of the sexual facts, his proximity to them had completely removed the more normal feelings of youngsters that the subject was naughty, dirty, wicked, taboo. It was like eating or drinking, and just as normal, but something you did not enjoy until you were married.

We pretty soon noticed that strict parental discipline was kept by the traditional boating families over their young, and respect was shown by the children for their parents. It occurred to me that the do-gooders, who are so keen to remove these youngsters from the boats for 'a proper education', would be far better occupied instructing parents in towns and cities in the all-important and difficult task of rearing children.

I do not suggest that the true boaters and their children are all perfect, but I maintain that they are a proud and happy race of fallible human beings with a reasonable working standard of morals, love of tradition, and respect for decent behaviour and for one another. During our career on the cut, we did hear of one shot-gun marriage. We heard the odd couple having a slanging match, but never of beatings or divorce. Perhaps the fact that husband and wife work together has some bearing on their relationship, for you cannot get too tough with the partner who is steering the other boat, and it's hard going if you have to work all the locks by yourself.

The reformers are horror-struck at the idea of young children sleeping in cabins with their parents. I maintain that this is a far more healthy way of learning about sex than that of the majority of children on the land. Land children are educated in small groups in playground corners, read pornographic novelettes, and watch films or plays of sex and violence in cinemas or the comfort of their homes. Meanwhile the parents are delighted because the little ones are quiet while they swop dirty stories at cocktail parties or enjoy the intellectual thrill of a bingo session.

Some would point out that John's statement, 'I would get killed, and so would she', if he were discovered playing round with a boater's daughter, illustrates that their code of ethics is maintained by fear. But at least they have a code, which is something, and is fear of physical punishment less worthy than fear of social ostracism or religious superstitions?

After lessons Gay and I went to the pub, while John joined friends on a pair recently moored behind us.

'Well, this is where it all started,' I remarked.

'What do you mean?'

'Here, in this bar, I met Albert Bishop. Strange that we have never come across him. I wonder if the landlord has seen him lately. They appeared to be pretty good friends.'

'Ask him.'

'I will sometime.'

'Whatever sort of conversation were you having with John? I've never heard so many Fs in such a short time.'

I told her of our talk, and outlined my feeling about morals on the cut.

'I must say you never see them behaving as people do in public on the land. I've watched them walking hand in hand, chasing one another and laughing together, all rather sweet really. But just think of the river-bank at Richmond on a nice summer evening. It is embarrassing to go for a stroll.'

'Indeed, anywhere will do these days—benches, shop porches, railway stations.'

'It's strange really. Never before has there been so much chance of education. It's now compulsory. School-leaving age is higher. Everyone has much more money. Yet delinquency flourishes. Why?'

I thought for a while and replied, 'I should say there are numerous reasons. The age lacks standards and has not yet learnt properly to use leisure. The Welfare State has made marriage and parenthood too easy. Materialism is a facile philosophy. Kids are disgusted by their elders, and get a kick out of shocking them. They are revolting against authority, which to them seems to have created an insecure and worthless society.'

'Well,' Gay remarked, 'I wonder if they will do any better. What do you think?'

'It would not surprise me to see the pendulum swing far in the opposite direction. An age may come which outdoes the Victorians in its less agreeable manifestations.'

'Yes, Sir. I don't know what you mean, but I'm sure you are right.'

I laughed. One cannot become too involved or serious in Gay's company. I tried to express my thoughts more simply, and said, 'What I mean is that probably all these long-haired, dirty, over-sexed little bastards will grow into pompous, prudish, Bible-punching parents, who will bash the fear of God and man into their offspring.'

'About time too,' she replied.

The landlord was swabbing his counter. I asked after Bishop.

'Oh him. Yes, poor fellow, I'm sorry for him. His wife had a nasty accident; broke a leg and two or three ribs. Now she has taken fright of canals. He's moored up the Wey or Kennet, I believe, living on the boats and doing nothing.'

'I'm sorry to hear that. Poor old Bishop. He dearly loved the cut.'

'It's always the women,' the landlord said, 'who have daft accidents. I've heard of many in my time here.'

I went back to Gay, who asked, 'What news?'

'Oh he's packed up. Living on his boats somewhere up the Thames.'

'Huh,' she grunted. 'Men, typical. They can never make up their minds. They are not positive like us women!'

'No, positive blooming nuisances.'

'Don't be rude. You couldn't do much without us anyway.'

* * * *

We were on our way early on Friday morning, working downwards through King's Langley, Watford, Rickmansworth and Uxbridge to Cowley. There were twenty-seven locks in twenty-two miles. At 4 in the afternoon we pulled into Dawley Dock, Stockley, less than two miles from the depôt at Bull's Bridge.

As always, Gay went off to the office to plead and charm the persons in charge into unloading us quickly. She returned with a promise for first thing on Saturday morning.

We appeared to be miles from anywhere. There was no point in cleaning the boats; so we lazed round on the cabin tops, talked, read, had an excellent meal and went early to sleep.

Bristowe-Tarvia were as good as their word. By 11.50 a.m. we were cleared. At 1 o'clock we were pulling backwards into the depôt.

The log of this trip makes interesting reading:

Leicester-Stanton-Stockley.	Moving.	76 hrs. 40 mins.
Distance.		184 miles.
Average m.p.h.		2·4.
Loading time.		1¾ hrs.
Unloading time.		3 hrs. 50 mins.
Cargo.	Slag.	51¼ tons.
Rate.		9/6d.
Into kitty.		£24 9 3d.

Remarks.

A little more efficiency on the cut, and we could make some money. Compare this trip with the preceding one, taking both from time of loading to time of unloading:

Milk powder.	10 days.	13/6d.	£27 6 9d.
Slag.	7 days.	9/6d.	£24 9 3d.

The slag rate is bad and the journey 23 miles longer, but the boaters were considered and the cargo mechanically handled.

Inland water transport could be a great asset to this country yet. Dredge the canals, bring back Number Ones, give boats a fair deal at depôts and wharves, install efficient machines for handling and there would be nothing to touch it. The roads, too, would be unburdened; but the right type of loads for rail and water must be selected. Water must take heavy-stock cargoes—copper, steel, coal, grain (not milk-powder, nor beef-powder, thank you).

It is interesting to compare with water transport the cost, number of men employed, capital involved and fuel expended in transporting 51¼ tons of slag from Stanton to Stockley by road or rail. Water transport is too slow, some say. Yet manufacturers should never be in a panic for their stock requirements unless they have made a mess of ordering. The cut could play a valuable rôle if someone with knowledge of it, belief in it and determination to see it properly used were put in command.

Thirty minutes after berthing our boats, we were on the way down to Brentford to load sugar in sacks for delivery to a Ministry of Food depôt near Marsworth, 40 miles away. It was an eighteen-hour trip for which they paid us eight shillings a ton—what we called 'a good 'un'.

So the spring passed, and at the end of our second three-month period I again brought our accounts up-to-date. The figures showed that we had carried 525 tons, earned £253 and expended £204, leaving a profit of £49. This, added to our original profit, gave us £73 in six months. A check on the log showed that we had been waiting, either for orders, or to be loaded or unloaded, for no fewer than 28 days — approximately one-third of the period.

'I must say we'll never get fat or retire on £146 profit a year. And we only want something to break and put us out of action for a bit and we've had it,' Gay commented.

'True,' I replied. And to discover her feelings about the life added, 'And of course there's the possibility of illness or accident. I wonder if we should give the game up, go back on the land and find ourselves a nice room somewhere, in Courtfield Gardens or Notting Hill. What do you think?'

'Oh no. Not bloody likely! We might do better in future. Don't be so easily discouraged! I don't know. Another Bishop! I told you way back that you men are not positive, not resolute.'

'You feel like carrying on then?'

'Of course I do. Meanwhile, we might see if we could squeeze higher rates out of them, or get our demural, demarriage, whatever you call it, raised.'

'That's an idea! Yes, we'll try that, although I rather doubt if we'll succeed. The boy seems happy enough, and we've the long summer days to come. We might do better.'

'Certainly we shall. Have you asked for orders?'

'Yes, but Mr Newbury wasn't optimistic. There are a good few pairs to load before our turn comes. Shall we go to Richmond? We can always ring up Newbury, and see how things are going.'

'Good idea. Oh for a bath and a long, long sleep. Oh, my God, what about John?'

'I've talked it over with him. All he wants are some cooking pots, our kettle and some money. Apparently the little blighter can cook as well as do everything else. He was surprised that I should worry about him, and said that anyway he'd be calling on his friends in the lay-by, and all would ask him to eat.'

'Oh good. That's a weight off my mind.'

'If I'm not mistaken, John will find his beloved Emma somewhere down this end of the cut.'

'She seems a nice kid, and I hope he pairs up with her sometime.'

It was an event which was to take place soon enough, and with disastrous results for ourselves.

PART THREE

Summer

CHAPTER IX

Buttying to Northampton with Wheat

'There's no doubt about it, Captain. Things is looking up on the cut. Dredgin' in the Parks. Cuttin' down some of those damned trees what over'ung the bends. Mendin' lock-gates what to my knowledge have been busted years. Can't make it out. Lengthsmen workin'. Even lock-keepers givin' one an 'and now and again. Bless my soul!' Steerer Flowers stuck his pipe-stem back between brown teeth.

'Something's abroad, right enough. What's more, they're pickin' on all the worsest places like as if they knew,' Boswell remarked.

'Not before time,' I said.

'You're right,' they echoed.

Not only was I right, but pleased. I was happy both to be among them yarning and to know that action was being taken as a result of my reports.

Apart from trying to earn a living on the cut, we were working for its improvement also. A senior official of the Executive had called us to his office. 'You did say you were one of the early members of the Inland Waterways Association, didn't you?'

'Yes, sir.'

'And something to do with the building trade?'

'Yes.'

'Then you could probably write reports on machinery, buildings, bridges, wharves and so on?'

'Certainly.'

'Good, good.' He was eager. He pulled his chair closer to his large desk, looked at me straight in the face and continued.

'Before nationalization of the waterways I was a company director. To be frank with you, I know little of what goes on out there in the docks, on the cuts. I am going to find out though. I am keen to make this section work efficiently, improve it, see that what little money is available is spent to the best advantage.' He pointed a pencil at me, and said, 'This is where you come in. I'm going to ask you to be my eyes and ears on the cut. I want reports from you on every aspect of the canals. Would you do that for me?'

I turned towards Gay. She was smiling, looking pleased. To me it was the most welcome request. I said as much.

'Good. There is to be nothing personal about these reports—no spying, only straightforward statements concerning every type of difficulty. Anything which, if put to rights, would help the boaters in their work, and make the waterways more efficient. You are the man for the job.'

So it came about that my log of each trip suddenly grew. I wrote of wharves where we could not come alongside because of mud, winding gear which was broken, serious cracks in the brickwork of bridges, trees which overhung our boats and swept chimneys, mops and water-cans into the cut, and so on in detail. It meant writing notes each day, and incorporating them in the log of every trip. In fact, it meant hours of extra work each week, but worth while. Every time we noticed action being taken as a result of our reports, we were pleased, and suddenly came to realize that our work, originally considered only as a move to improve the waterways, was directly benefiting ourselves. It was agreed that we should speak to nobody about these activities. That was why I enjoyed this conversation with Flowers and Boswell so much. I felt that at last we were contributing something to this small but beloved community, and to a branch of England's beautiful waterways. It was a good feeling.

Today everything was good. We were real boaters now, accepted anywhere in that company. The word 'trainees' had left our world. We worked harder than most, and held our own with any of them where boating was concerned. Today we had scrubbed out. The cabin roofs were littered with drawers and utensils drying in the hot July sun. The brass was gleaming; our ropework, scrubbed clean, was drying. Gay was in Southall shopping, while I stood chatting with friends and listening for our name to be called on the P.A. system.

John, of whom we were both very fond, had filled out and changed quite a bit during the months with us. He had matured, but had remained unaffected by his gain of a little knowledge. He could now read simple books and write some kind of hand, but still he found it difficult to hold, and make letters with, anything so small and brittle as a pen or pencil. As well as teaching him the Rs, I had talked to him for hundreds of hours about worthwhile things, human qualities — intellect, imagination, anger, fear and so on. In talking I found advantages to myself, for I had to sort, clear and assemble my own ideas, and express them clearly in simple terms. In fact, I learnt something of the problem of teaching.

His love affair with Emma went smoothly from strength to strength, and our letters to her had become quite lyrical. To each that I penned John now added something of his own, which I did not see. But it amused me vastly, when a letter was being written, to be asked 'How do you spell gorjus?' and other rather personal words. At times I couldn't imagine what he was writing to her about.

Just now John was in Brentford with his Emma, while her pair was loaded with lime-juice in casks. This was great good fortune for him, and it seldom happened. With our pairs ceaselessly on the move, the young people had small chance of a spell together. Usually their meetings consisted of a chat by a lock or for an hour or two of an evening in a lay-by. Courting on the cut was a difficult, chancy game, mostly made up of snatched minutes and letters.

'Steerers Phelps and Fern to the office, please.'

Good. That's what I had been waiting to hear. No rushing these days. Phelps came ashore and together we ambled to the office.

'What this time, I wonder,' he remarked.

'We'll find out soon enough. I don't know about you, but a couple of days in the depôt is enough for me. I like to be on the move.'

'You should. You're a Number One. I don't mind a break and a few evenings in "The Navigation" with me mates. Anyway me kid's ill, and I was hoping to get Doctor Smith to him. Seems as if we'll have to go without.'

Mr Newbury was on the phone. 'Hold on a minute,' he whispered. Phelps and I talked together. Then, 'You two run in double harness?' Mr Newbury asked.

'Yes. Captain and me are old mates,' Phelps said.

'Good. There's a hundred tons of wheat in Brentford for delivery to Westley's, Northampton. Load tomorrow morning and butty one another. How's that son of yours, Jim?'

'Poorly, I'd say.'

'Well, look after him, and, if he gets worse, push on up to Stoke Bruerne and have Sister Mary look at him. Tie up if needs be. Take no chances, mind.'

'I'll do that. Good-day to you then.'

We left the office. 'Decent chap Newbury,' Phelps remarked.

'What's he mean "Run in double harness? Butty one another?" I never heard the expressions.'

He laughed, and replied, 'You're a young' un really. You belong to the time of motors, whereas I belong more to horses. To run in double harness means to be mates, to get along together. Buttying just means like when there's a small cargo—in this case a hundred tons. So we load and do the journey together, helping one another with lock-work and suchlike. ' 'Tis all right if you and the other steerer gets along good together. You and me'll have some fine yarns. Likewise your missis and mine and Violet.'

'Oh grand. I'm pleased. What's the road like from Gayton?'

'Proper bugger. Bow hauling most of the way. By the time we get to Westley's you'll know what it was to be a horse. When shall us leave?'

'Soon as my missis comes back.'

'Right, Jim. Give us the word.' He ambled along the hard to his pair. I had noticed the 'Jim' and was pleased. Evidently he meant us to run really smoothly in double harness, and I meant the same. We had met a few times before, way back in our earliest days at Fenny. In fact he was the steerer who had found young John for us. This trip should be fun.

As soon as Gay returned I said, 'Come on, girl. We're going buttying.'

She looked at me, smiled and said, 'You're excited about something. What's happened since I've been away?'

I told her. She said pointedly, 'Good job I cleaned our holds so well after the last trip. If I'm not mistaken, we are inspected before loading grain.'

'Cleaning house is a woman's task. Yes, they inspect the

holds; then issue vast white sheets, which we rig so that the cargo does not spill away beneath the floorboards. Phelps will show us how to do this, but John will know anyway.'

We seemed to fly down to Brentford with Gay, Violet and the lock-keepers working us through. The dock was crowded, but we spotted John helping the Bucks to sheet-up. Both he and Emma waved. Our pairs were tied up alongside one another, our two on the inside. Soon after mooring, we heard Jim Phelps bellowing, 'May we cross?'

I looked out. He and his wife were up the fore end, and both carried shopping baskets. They were off to the village for stores. 'Go ahead,' I called.

John arrived looking happy. I gave him our news, enquired about Emma, and finally said, 'When the Phelps went ashore just now, they must have troubled to walk right up for'ard of their boats before asking if they could cross. Is this always done?'

'My dad always does. So does I. But some don't. It's the right thing really. Same as you never walk up to the back end of a boat and look in the cabin, but knocks, up on the side. If you want to be right, Captain, you'll cross by the fore end, and ask —if anyone's around to ask.'

'That's pleasant,' I remarked. 'Good manners. I like it.'

'We always does it. I'm going to check my engine now. Then I'll draw the sheets from the office.'

'Can you get some for Phelps?'

'Of course,' he said. 'I'll do that.' The tone of his voice made me feel that I had asked a stupid question. Evidently this buttying business was going to teach us a few more facts of boaters' etiquette.

At about 9 a.m. the following day we moved into position alongside a lighter. Two cranes fitted with grabs began loading our boats. Already I had a poor opinion of the mechanical handling equipment used on the cut, and this experience did nothing to improve it.

The grabs had no doubt been used to pick up various types of cargo. Their teeth were worn and ill-fitting. The buckets were raised while over-filled, and swung in an arc over the cut. Wheat shot out of the top at the beginning of the arc, and poured in golden falls from gaps between the teeth, down into the water, during the arc. On every lift some pounds of grain were lost, and to load our pairs took hundreds of lifts. This, in 1949, when rationing was still in force in England, and millions of people were starving in other parts of the world! It made me angry to see such waste and inefficiency.

It took 4 hours 50 minutes to load our pair, and our gauged weight was 50½ tons. Gay as usual seized the rates book, and read out, 'Wheat, Brentford - Northampton, 8s 9d per ton. What a sum! I must do it on paper.'

'You wait, you old miser. Come and help to sheet-up. There are four boats now, remember.'

'Oh, of course, Jimmy, but I do like to know how much one is going to earn. It helps me to work more willingly.'

We left Brentford at 2.30 p.m., Phelps leading, the four boats strung in a long line down the cut. Violet joined Gay in our butty, immediately took the tiller and ceaselessly chatted away. Gay sat on the roof of the cabin. Violet had the typical style of women steerers—arms crossed, body leaning downwards on the great wooden handle, taking weight off her legs, relaxed. They looked as if they were both enjoying a restful holiday. John sang, turned a few somersaults over his tiller and was obviously happy to be following his beloved Emma up the cut. Phelps pushed ahead, flat out, while his wife leant on her tiller, now looking ahead, now into the cabin to watch her sick child. I rode up the towpath ahead of them, set the locks ready, warned them to slow down if the road was not clear, or signalled them on.

At Norwood Top I went aboard, stowed the bicycle, and joined John on our motor-boat, as it was six miles to the next lock at Cowley. We were doing well. I was daring to think that this might be a good, quick trip, when suddenly Phelps's engine revolutions fell. He took the usual action on these occasions, closed the throttle, engaged reverse, opened the throttle and gave the propeller a chance to throw off anything which might be entwined around it. Then he went ahead again, but still the revs. did not rise. He signalled us to come abreast. I leapt for his cabin top, John dropped astern again, and while I took over his tiller he shot down into the engine-room. He was quickly back. 'Union gone at fuel pump. We'll have to pull into the depôt.'

'O.K. It's six o'clock anyway,' I said.

'Hell. They'll all be gone by the time we get there.'

We didn't get away until nearly noon next day. The road was cluttered with barges and lighters as so often down London end, and by eight that night we had reached only Kings Langley. During the day their child had, they thought, become rapidly worse.

'Have you taken his temperature?' I asked, quite forgetting that these people were boaters.

'Temperature? No. I got nothing to do that with.'

'I have. Would you like us to look at him? See what we can do?'

'Please, Captain. Yes, that would be good.' He called into his butty, 'Missis, tidy the place up. Captain's coming to look at Kim. Vi, help your mother. Maybe you'd know what's up.'

He brightened, and seemed pleased by my suggestion.

Always, on our butty, we carried a full first-aid kit. In the Army I had been through a fairly intensive medical course, but it was concerned more with wounds than disease. However, I felt sure that at least we could do the child no harm. We went into their butty. It was stiflingly hot, all the ventilation having been carefully closed. I noticed that it was spotless.

The child was nervous at first. His forehead and hands were damp. He had a pain in his stomach, and had been sick. I gently pressed the left side of his abdomen below his navel and asked, 'Does that hurt, Kim?' He thought for a moment. I pressed him again. 'No,' he said. Next, and nervously, I repeated the test on the right side. 'No, it doesn't hurt.'

'Good. Now, Kim, open your mouth. See just how far you can open it, and don't bite me.'

His throat was inflamed, his breathing rough, his temperature 102°.

We all climbed from the butty and joined Phelps on the tow-path. 'What you make of it then?' he asked.

'Well, understand this. I'm no doctor, but my guess is influenza or a bad cold in the head and stomach. He has pain there, but not in the appendix. Has he got diarrhoea, Mrs Phelps?'

'Yes. Come on today it did. Very loose I'd say myself.'

'Oh, well, that will be it.' I stood thinking for a moment. Phelps said, 'What do we do? Can you say? Do you know?'

'A doctor should see him really,' Gay suggested.

'No doctor will come here,' Mrs Phelps said.

'Oh yes he will. I could go and find one; bring him here to the boats.'

'No,' Phelps said. 'Our doctor is Doctor Smith in Southall. He knows us people. He understands us. Others always say, "Take the child off the boat. He must go to hospital".'

'How long are we from Sister Mary?' I asked.

'Two days. He'll be all right for two days now surely? Sister Mary's a good one. She'll see him proper,' his wife remarked.

'As you wish.'

'Anything we can do for him now, Captain?' Phelps asked.

'Yes. To begin with, let the range out, and cook on the motor-boat. Open all the ventilators, and let some fresh air into your butty. Give him no more solid food. Liquids only—milk, barley water. We'll get that from the town immediately. And broth. Have you any meat?'

'A little,' Mrs Phelps replied.

'Good. Now, before you do these things, sponge him down, change his pyjamas, crush this aspirin in hot milk and give it to him, and feed these throat pastilles to him every now and then.'

'Thank you ever so. It's real good of you, but are you sure about the air?' Mrs Phelps looked worried.

'Oh yes. Fug breeds germs. Open the place up, especially in this lovely weather. Give him oxygen, the more the better.'

'Oxygen?' she repeated, and smiled as if suddenly understanding, or filled with admiration for my profound knowledge. Then she jumped aboard saying, 'Oxygen, that'll do it. Come on Vi. Give us a hand.'

Gay and I walked into the town, and had the luck to find a chemist's shop open. Here we purchased barley water, Benger's and meat extracts. John had borrowed the bicycle, and gone charging up the cut, without food, to look for Emma.

While the womenfolk were preparing a meal, Phelps and I sat on a balance beam enjoying the beautiful evening and talking.

'Why,' I asked him, 'do you have this distrust of people on the land? Why would you not let me bring a doctor to Kim?'

'Must seem strange to you, I suppose. Fact is, those people look down their noses on the likes of us. We have our people and shops ashore what are used to us, what I use like me father did afore. Mostly they're all kind and help us. Rationing, I ask you. What's a ration card to the likes of us?'

'I can understand that, of course, but what about this doctor business?'

'We all have one big fear, which is being took off our boats. A doctor on the land don't understand how we live. The boat is our home but company's property. They must be on the move always. Then there's the cargo in 'em to think of.'

'Who is this Doctor Smith you speak about?'

'Ah, he's different. He's jannock. He's the boater's doctor. Knows all about us; understands. He'd give us medicine and a note for Sister Mary at Stoke. She'd see how things were. She understands too. All of us trusts Doctor Smith, and know that if he says, "To hospital," well that's it. But he'd never say so lightly. He's brought hundreds of boaters' kids into this world, and seen a few of the old 'uns on their way in his time. Good man, one of the best to us.'

'These shops of yours, do you never use any other?'

'Oh yes, up country, Woolworths and that. They're all right, but my missis and Vi have sometimes been told to get out. "No gipsies served in here," say some shops. It hurts, you know. We are poor people but proud, and, anyway, after being insulted so often, we kind of go into our shells like, if you follow me. We don't stick out our necks asking them to be beat.'

'Why ever should anybody take your wife and Violet, who is fair, for gipsies?'

'Ah. It's because they wear boots, see.'

Later that night we gave Kim another crushed aspirin, and settled him comfortably. His temperature was 102·4°, which worried me, but Gay said, 'Kids of his age are inclined to run high temperatures when they are ill. I shouldn't worry too much.'

'But it's a hell of a responsibility we're taking. A doctor should see him.'

'Look, that is up to his parents. We can only do our best. So stop worrying and get some sleep. We'll see how he is in the morning.'

* * * *

We were dressed by four the following morning. Later Mrs

K

Phelps tapped on the side of our cabin. 'He's better,' she said excitedly. 'I'm sure he's better. Slept like something dead, he did. I stayed awake nearly all night just in case, but it wasn't till half-past five that he woke.'

'We'll come over directly. Don't give him anything meanwhile.'

'Lord bless you, Captain. You're a good one.'

The child's temperature was 100·8°. His throat was still sore, and now his nose was running, a fact which pleased me. We taught him to gargle, fed him on Benger's, gave him another aspirin, made his bed, and told both him and Mrs Phelps to get some sleep. Violet closed the cabin doors, opened the hatch in the roof and took the helm. John and Gay handled our boats. I lock-wheeled. We cast off at 6.35 a.m., and with everything going well worked our way up the long climb towards Cowroast.

As usual, this was too good to last. I bicycled around a sharp corner. Ahead was a lock; beyond it an almost empty pound with a strip of water about four feet wide lying along the bottom. To right and left of the strip lay the fantastic assortment of junk which landsmen throw in the cut. Bicycle wheels predominated, with pots, pans, car-batteries, a crushed pram, the frame of a motor-cycle, enough metal rubbish to stock a yard. Never before had I experienced this. I didn't even know what to do; so, turning about, I sped down the towpath to Phelps.

The answer to this problem was the same as that which we had learnt upon our first trip—borrowing water from pounds above. As a result we suffered from low pounds all the way to the summit, and the very day which we hoped would bring us so much nearer to Stoke Bruerne and Sister Mary was ruined. We punched along for twelve hours through thirty-six locks, covering sixteen miles only with an average of 1⅓ miles an hour.

However, Kim was better, and the thermometer that evening registered 100·2°. Mrs Phelps had slept. Gay and I felt some relief. Phelps and Violet looked more cheerful. John alone was displeased because his Emma, who had tied up well above the empty pound on the previous night, would now be many miles ahead of us.

'How does a thing like that empty pound happen?' I asked Phelps, as we sat smoking and enjoying the evening.

'Two causes really, both bloody carelessness. Either someone closes the top gates, and doesn't notice a wedge is caught between them. Or, like so many, they let the paddles drop, but don't check that they have gone right down. Either way there's a constant leak, which during all of a night will empty a pound.'

We heard Violet screaming. Phelps looked round in the direction of our pair, and watched his daughter wrestling with John on the roof of 'Bawtry's' cabin. Violet, who usually appeared so demure, and was just one day short of her twentieth birthday, was fighting like a tomboy. They looked like a couple of ten-year-olds. John at last had her down on her back. He was sitting astride her, leaning over the edge, dunking a mop in the cut. It seemed as if Violet was going to get wet.

'Steady there, you two. Break it up,' Phelps bellowed.

They did so immediately. Violet, moving to the end of the roof, sat with her legs swinging up and down above the cockpit. John spun the mop dry, and replaced it with its head pointing for'ard, its handle resting in the looped handle of the Buckby water-can. Then he sat with his back against Violet. They continued laughing and chatting together.

This scene quite suddenly made me realize how much like brothers and sisters were all the boater's children, even those quite unrelated. Their world is small. They grow up meeting one another in the same places year in, year out; playing together on hards, wharves and towpaths.

Gay and Mrs Phelps sat one either side of the upswept tiller of the Phelps's butty, deep in conversation.

'What brought you to the cut?' Phelps suddenly asked me.

I told him some of my story.

'Can't think how life would be if a man didn't care for his job,' he remarked. Then he added, 'People like me, Buck, Garside, Skinner, Flowers — you knows 'em now, we old timers — we reckons to die on our boats. What haunts me is the thought of an accident like Vokins had. You must have seen him down Brentford, a metal hook stuck on the end of his right arm. Had his wrist crushed between two moving boats what was breasting. Finished him it did.'

'But he's still working. He's by the cut, among boaters.'

'By it, yes, but not on it. Gone dour he has, withered. Yes, that's it seemingly. Take us off our boats, and we withers like a picked flower.'

'I've been trying to explain these things to young John, but it is difficult with kids. He thinks that life ashore must be better. It is my belief that, if he found himself working day in, day out, on a factory floor, at some unskilled task, he would soon wither also.'

'Even since before I wed Sarah—that's my missis—I've had a purpose in mind. A peaceful life, doing my work good and well, a family of me own. So it has come about, but now I want Vi married and on the land, and young Kim brought up strong. Then away off the cut for his learning.'

'Why do you wish the children to go on the land?'

'The cut will see me out, but it's finished. We've watched it dying; seen great roads come to the country we pass through, and the number of pairs going down and down. Just now, under this nationalization, a bit is happening, but it's wind mostly. There's not the men to dredge, and neither the money nor machinery to put things to rights. We're doomed, I reckon, and in a few years what's left of the cut will be like a kid's pond—just covered with a lot of toy boats running around amusing themselves.'

'I hope you are wrong,' I said, 'for it is my belief that the canals of England can still play a useful rôle.'

'Could, you mean. Sure enough, they could if handled right. Bless me, I remember working the Kennet and Avon. Wide you know, wide all the way. None of this lark we got to face down Northampton Arm. They tell me the K. & A. is finished. You ask Mr Newbury. He's the man on canals. Reads all the books. Know's what's on. Anyway, there are not the men any more. Now you, for instance. You won't stay on the cut, will you?'

'No, I came for a purpose, as I've told you. I shall leave in time, but when I do I shall know what I'm talking about, and my aim will be to fight hard for the preservation of the canals, the improvement of them, and better conditions for those who are still working on them. You take my extra cabin, for instance. It has proved itself to be no handicap, and think what it would mean to boaters if they all had that much extra accommodation. "You've ruined a good boat," they all said. Have I hell? With the simple addition of slack boards I carry as much as any of you.

'The longer I am on the cut,' I went on, 'the more certain I am about its sicknesses. The troubles are caused by mixing up barges, lighters and narrow boats on the lengths near London. Then there is not enough mechanical handling equipment at docks and wharves, with complete lack of modern machinery for dredging, and the inefficiency or laziness of so many lock-keepers and lengthmen.'

'That, Captain, is saying a mouthful. But, bless me, in the time you been on, you certainly have done your best to find out. Point is, what can you do about it?'

'I don't know, but I'll find out.'

We tied up in the basin at the top of Stoke Bruerne Flight the following evening. Kim had continued to recover, and to everyone's delight Sister Mary pronounced him on the mend. My diagnosis had been right—more by luck than knowledge—and my treatment satisfactory as far as it went. Sister Mary congratulated me, and I felt immensely happy. She gave further instructions and a box of pills to Mrs Phelps. Henceforward I backed out of the responsibility, glad to be rid of it, pleased to have been of some help.

We celebrated in the 'Boat' that night. Kim was fast asleep. John did not want to come, and agreed to stay near the Phelps's boat just in case the child woke up and needed anything. It was Violet's twentieth birthday, and for the occasion she wore shoes, stockings and a colourful short-sleeved cotton dress. Her long fair hair shone in the evening sunlight. She had some make-up on her rather broad but handsome face; and a pair of red ear-rings, which somehow suited her well, dangled and jumped. I had never seen her turned out like this before, and, as she had been for some time in our butty, I guessed that Gay was to a certain extent responsible. Somehow the ear-rings struck a chord of memory.

Mrs Phelps looked at her daugher, and enquired, 'What have you got on your face, child?'

'It's Gay, mum. She did it for me. And look at these. Aren't they lovely?' She shook her head from side to side, and the ear-rings flashed beneath the flying cloud of fair hair. 'Gay has given me these for a birthday present, my first ear-rings.'

She now not only looked attractive, but was obviously radiantly happy. The thought crossed my mind that we were, without a doubt, running well in double harness with all the Phelpses.

Soon the womenfolk were seated and deep in conversation. Phelps and I stood at the counter.

'I was pleased, at last, to meet Sister Mary. She is an impressive person—kind, gentle and firm too, I should think. Do you know her well?'

'I'll say. Brought both our kids into the world; looked after Sarah when she had her second miscarriage. Sister Mary is all right. Always wears that long white thing on her head, and you should see her house, so clean and shining a body hardly dares go in. On the walls pictures of bones and all of a man's guts. Quite frightening it is. But she knows everything, and does everything to help the likes of we. She's our nurse, doctor and friend, all in that small body under the white hat. You know she even helps to set the locks, and can wind a paddle, but she says winding paddles isn't a woman's work, leastwise not when she's heavy. "Jim Phelps," she said to me when Kim was in the oven but soon due, "you will not allow your wife to wind any more paddles until I say you may. Understand, man?" I was quite scared. She looked me in the eye like as to say, "I'll know if you do, and the good Lord help you for you'll be in some trouble." I didn't dare let Sarah hardly do a thing, and in due time we was back. Sister Mary set the lock, leant on the beam so to speak, and brings Kim through, bellowing his nut off like a good 'un. Yes, I always says, "God bless Sister Mary". She's real good.'

We had a great evening, lots of beer, and music from an accordion, really well played by an old boater with a long flowing white moustache and smart navy-blue trilby hat, which he raised every time we clapped his tunes. We sang sad old songs like 'Goodbye Old Ship of Mine', and Phelps taught us how to play 'Threes and Fives' with dominoes. We stayed until closing time, and even then stood talking in the beautiful cool air of the July night, not giving a thought to our alarms already set for 4 a.m.

Back in our butty I said to Gay, 'Wherever did you get those ear-rings?'

'Aunt Mary of course. She always sends me some useless piece of cheap jewellery at Christmas, and fortunately I hadn't thrown them away as I usually do.'

'What a bit of luck. In a wild kind of way they suited Violet, and didn't she love them?'

'The kid cried when I gave them to her. She's terribly emotional and intense. She has asked me to take her shopping for a dress in Northampton. Says she wouldn't dare go alone. I asked her why not, and do you know what she replied?'

'No what?'

'She said she is frightened that sales-girls will be unkind to her, as she has heard them be to her mother. She has even paid for and run out of shops with things which wouldn't fit her, because the woman serving was sharp.'

'Poor kid. You'll take her of course.'

'I will, and God help any counter skipper who is unkind to her while I'm around.'

* * * *

We let go from Stoke top at 6.30 a.m. and an hour later turned right on to the Northampton Arm, and began what amounted to five miles of absolute hell. There are seventeen narrow locks on this stretch, and finally one wide guillotine lock which opens on to the River Nene. Through fourteen of the narrow locks we had to bow-haul the two butties. On the other three, Phelps and John worked a clever trick by which they towed the butties through using the long cotton bow-hauling line.

We worked the two motor-boats down the flight first; then tied them up, and returned to the top, where we hitched the cotton line to the mast of Phelps's butty. We began the task of heaving her along by hand, one man ahead with the line looped over a shoulder, the other two spaced along the line and hauling it. The women did the lock work. To say that this was hard slow going is an understatement. It takes some mighty great heaving to pull a 70-feet hull, with 25 tons of cargo aboard, out of a lock into which it fits snugly. Starting the boats was the greatest difficulty. Once they were under way there was little to it. Having joined Phelps's butty to his motor, we then tramped back up the hill, and repeated the whole performance with 'Bawtry'.

The whole arm was little more than a muddy ditch choked with reeds and weeds, which reduced its original width by about half. On arrival at the guillotine lock, we found it chained. We walked to the lock-keeper's house, and were told that he was out and had the key with him. Our cup of bitterness was full to the brim. We had risen early and worked fast and hard, only to find ourselves locked out when almost in sight of our destination.

My log for this day reads:

7½ hrs. 10 miles. 18 locks.
Average 1·3 m.p.h.

The unloading at Westley's Mill made an interesting comparison with the loading at Brentford. First, we drew in under cover so that work could proceed whatever the weather, for wheat must not get wet. Then a roaring din started somewhere within the mill, and a cheerful fellow appeared carrying a large flexible pipe, which he threw into the mass of grain. At the same time he bellowed at me, 'Sit on that bugger, mate, and keep it well down. Feed it like. The better you do that, the sooner we'll be through. O.K.?' Then the roar increased as the revolutions of the sucking mechanism rose. The pipe came to life, and started trying to lash about like a live python. I wrestled with it at first, but quickly learnt how to keep it wedged and under control. A hole formed in the wheat. Gradually it became a valley, and the sweet-smelling golden grain cascaded down the slopes into the hungry mouth of the python. Towards the finish we cup-shaped the white sheets, so that every grain was sucked into the mill, and nothing was wasted. It was a neat example of efficient mechanical handling of cargo.

Gay, Violet and John went shopping in Northampton. Sarah Phelps cleaned her cabins and nursed Kim, who was much better and demanding food. But his temperature was not yet normal, and I advised against solids. Jim Phelps and I juggled the boats around, and took turns at controlling the python and going ashore for a smoke. Conversation was impossible. Everything was suggested in sign language.

In the evening Violet and John went to a cinema, but the Phelpses stayed aboard. Gay and I visited a pub, which Jim said was the brightest in Northampton and all the boaters used it. It was gay; noisy with bustle, laughter and music. There were a number of rough-looking men and distinctly tarty women in it, but all were friendly. We had a good session on the dart-board, winning, losing, being stood and standing drinks accordingly. The whole atmosphere was friendly and happy.

Gay was on the throw when a man came up to her and said quietly, 'I shouldn't leave your bag there if I were you. It might disappear.'

'Oh, thank you, but don't worry. There's nothing valuable in it.' She smiled at him, and threw a lovely group of twenties, making a nice round ton which brought a roar of applause from the onlookers.

The next day we called at the British Waterways office for orders. Phelps was to report to Hawkesbury and load coal; we to Tyseley. The manager here seemed to know all about us, and asked friendly questions. We had quite a long talk with him, during which I complained about the condition of the Arm and the locking of the guillotine lock. He agreed to see what he could do about these troubles. We told him of our splendid evening in the pub. He looked surprised, and said, 'You two in there? Lord, I wonder you got out alive.'

'What do you mean? It's a wonderful spot, and full of the most friendly people. A bit rough perhaps, but good sorts.'

'For your information, that pub is infamous. It is the haunt of all the thugs, petty criminals and ladies of easy virtue in Northampton. The police leave it alone because it is remote from the centre of the city, and they know where to find any of the bad characters they might want to question.'

When Gay and I returned to Westley's, we found the boats winded and both butty cratches down.

'Hell,' I complained. 'That's a nuisance. Did we have to do that? Was there no chance of passing under those bridges with them up?'

'Not a hope,' Phelps answered. 'We've tried it before. They had to come down. You'll see.'

'I'll never get mine back up as neatly as it was.'

'Maybe you wouldn't, Captain, but I will. Just you wait and see.' John looked quite offended.

'We'll fix it neat and proper,' Phelps agreed.

I smiled at them both, and remarked, 'I'm sorry. That was rude of me. I'm sure you will. I was only remembering what a dreadful mess I made of it myself.'

'That's all right, Captain,' Phelps said, and added, 'You can't learn to do everything right in a few months. Matey here and I been at it years.'

We worked our way back up the Northampton Arm at a tremendous speed, Violet, Mrs Phelps and Gay aboard the boats and we three men really going hard. It was a brilliant day. A fresh cooling breeze blew. We each had our tasks. The work was efficient, quietly but speedily done. I found it exhilarating to be a member of the team, and enjoyed every moment of it—except my turn of bow hauling, for this seemed, more than anything I had done on the cut, to strain my damaged neck and shoulder.

At Gayton, on the main route again, we turned right, and flew along the 12½ miles pound to Buckby, forked left at Norton, and blasted our way through the 2,000 yards of the Braunston Tunnel. We plummeted down Braunston's six locks, and tied up at the parting of the ways, having worked 31 locks and travelled 22 miles without any kind of hold-up. A glorious end to our happy experience of buttying.

But these experiences were not yet finished. As usual we both examined and put our engines to sleep. Next, the four boats were mopped down, and the gear on the cabin roofs—long and short shafts, mops, dippers, Buckby cans, and side straps—were cleaned and arranged neatly all in their traditional places. Then the task of building the cratches began. These cratches are at the fore end of the holds, and look very like large sentry boxes. But the roof, instead of ending in an apex, is flattened to the width of the top-plank, which rests on them when the holds are sheeted. They are almost, but not quite, the full width of the boats, for when they are in position a gunwale about three inches wide remains exposed. They are planked first; then covered neatly with folded black tarpaulin similar to the sheets. This is tacked in position, and then roped with three equally-spaced sets of triple white cotton line. The ends of these are finally rolled in scrolls, and tucked beneath the three lines. Inside the cratch, at gunwale level, is a wide beam or shelf on which the sheets rest when the boats are empty. It is difficult even to describe a cratch, but to build and finish them as attractively as good boaters do is a work of art.

I stood and watched. Jim Phelps and John worked and talked incessantly about the job. Sarah Phelps came along, examined their work, and exclaimed, 'Jim Phelps, *that* will never do. You got a crease here. Look. Must have a tuck in under there someplace. Lift it, lift it, man.' She pushed her thin arm up under the tarpaulin and shoved, working the hard folded material flat.

'Come on, woman. Come out of it. We've got a job to do,' Phelps complained.

'Bide a while, man, and it will look proper.' She withdrew her arm, patted the surface, and said, 'Now that's better'. Then she winked at me.

'How's Kim this evening?' I asked.

'Oh fine. Worrying to be up. Says his belly aches, but not like before. He wants vittles all the time.'

'I'll take his temperature again directly, and if it is normal tonight, and tomorrow morning, you could let him get up tomorrow and into the sun. Keep him still—no running around. Two or three hours only about noon. You can start to build him up now. Give him all the milk you can buy.'

'I'll do that, and thank you.' She put her hand on my arm, squeezed it and continued, 'Thank you ever so. And I want to pay you for the medicines you got for 'im.'

'No, don't worry about that. Think of it as a little present from us to Kim.'

'We must . . . ' she began.

'Look. I'd much rather you didn't. It was very little. We would like you to leave it this way—a present for the lad. But just one thing I want you to promise me. I've shown you how a thermometer works. You remember the red line at "normal" now, don't you?'

'Oh yes, and shaking it.'

'Well, promise me that you will buy one, and keep it safely on the boats, always.'

'I promise, and I said it afore and say it now again, God bless you, Captain.'

She turned away and walked hurriedly to her butty. I stood looking at the brave, frail, clean little woman, and thought of Kim, Vi with her childish delight in the ear-rings, Jim working so carefully on my cratch, And a feeling of love for these people swamped me.

Later, after we had had our supper, we heard a gentle knocking on our cabin's side.

'Who is there?'

' 'Tis me, Vi. Can I come in?'

'Of course, Violet. Come aboard.' I rose to help her, as she was carrying something wrapped in newspaper in one hand. Gay and I pushed up along the side bed to make room for her to sit down. Our small table, which folded upwards to close the crocks cupboard, was still down but had been cleared. Now she rested her parcel gently on this table and said, 'These is for you'. Then she rose and started up the steps into the steering cockpit.

'Come back, Vi,' I called, but she continued on her way. I shot from the cabin, and caught hold of her as she was stepping over the gun'ale to the towpath. She tried to shake me off, but I held her tightly, and was amazed by her strength and the hardness of her arm.

'Come back, Vi. Come and show us what you have brought. Don't go away so soon.'

She stopped fighting. I helped her back into the cabin, and she sat between us.

'Go on. Undo it.'

'They're for you. You undo it.' She pushed the parcel towards Gay, who unwrapped it carefully and placed two beautiful china side-plates on the table.

I have them here now and must describe them. Each is six inches in diameter, fine white china with a narrow line of gold painted round the rim. From here for about one inch towards the middle of the plate, the china is like open lace. Eight differently coloured and shaped hand-painted flowers come next, equally spaced; then another circle of narrow gold. Within this circle are painted clusters of variously-coloured flowers, interspersed with leaves of subtly different shades of green, the stalks and stems of each group leading in natural curves to the next. These flowers are blue, pink, violet and mauve, and, of course, the largest flower of each group is a pale red rose. In the centre of the back of each plate is a moulded boss, with a hole through it large enough to take a piece of twine. For this ware is too precious and beautiful to stack in any cupboard. It is hung in the cabins where it can be admired, and, when the boats are rammed by barges or lighters, it swings safely from hooks. I knew at the time of giving that this china was no longer made. It was already sought by collectors. It was priceless.

We both gazed at the plates; then lifted and admired them. We thought not only how they might adorn our cabin, but also how impossible it was to accept such a valuable gift from the Phelpses. I said, 'Thank you, my dear Violet. They really are the most beautiful plates I have ever seen. But we can't accept them. They are very valuable, my dear. You mustn't give them away ever, and certainly not to us who have done nothing to deserve them.'

She did not speak, but just sat with her face downcast, her shining hair tumbled over her shoulders, masking her expression. Gently I wrapped the plates and moved them across the table towards her. Then she turned towards me, tears glistening in her eyes, and said quietly, 'They're not good enough for all you have done. You must take them. Mum and dad want you to have them for your home. We've got lots. These were hid under the bed—really.'

'Look Vi, even if that is true, you mustn't give them away. You could sell them for a lot of money in London, anywhere. They're really valuable.'

She was crying now, mopping large shining tears from her pretty face. Gay put an arm round Violet's shoulder, and immediately the child broke down, buried her head in Gay's chest, cried, talked and mopped, all at the same time. Then the terrible remark came. 'They are not good enough for you, but they are all we had.'

Now we really were in a fix. I thought for a few moments, while Gay nursed and talked to Vi as if she were a small baby. She was trying once again to explain how we felt that we would be accepting, too readily, a priceless gift.

'Vi,' I said, 'look at me for a moment. Come on. Head up. Good girl. Now, stop crying. Mop those tears away. Sit up and look pretty again.' I spoke quite firmly, and she reacted as if she had been given a fierce order.

'Come on. Smile. Let's see that smile of yours.' She sat up, smiled, dabbed once or twice, and pulled herself together. I continued, 'We'd dearly love to have these plates. We'll take them now. But you must tell your parents what I said about their value and selling them. Then, tomorrow, if they are absolutely sure they want us to keep them, we will. How lovely they are! Where should we hang them? Come on. What do you say?'

It was all over immediately. She rose and started an eager conversation with Gay about exactly where and how they should be placed. We all talked for quite a long time before Violet finally left, looking happy and pretty again.

Soon after five next morning we were ready to go our separate ways. I strolled along to Phelps's butty, knocked, climbed aboard, tickled Kim in the ribs, and said, 'Right. Open it.' He giggled and swung his head from side to side in flat refusal. It was a game. I had not yet said the all-important piece which he liked to hear.

'Come on. I want to see if the engine's at the right temperature. Open up there.'

He was normal.

We all stood in a group talking while our diesels warmed up, and feeling—at least it was certainly so in our case—sad to be parting. To Phelps I said, 'Jim, did Violet tell you all I said about those wonderful plates?'

'About them being valuable and so on, you mean?'

'Yes, exactly that. You shouldn't give them to us. I have them wrapped. I want you, quietly, to take them back, and don't say a word to Vi or your Sarah.'

'Real valuable, are they?'

'Yes, without any doubt.'

We were moving towards our butty. I was about to step aboard when he clutched my shoulder, and said, 'The more valuable they is, the better pleased I be. They're for you and your missis. Thanks for what you done.' He extended his great horny hand. We shook. 'Goodbye, mate. You'll do. Have a good trip.' He turned away, and began to cast off his lines.

We stood waving and yelling 'goodbyes' as they drew away, heading for Hawkesbury and the coalfields round Coventry. I blew kisses at Sarah and Violet. They blew others back. We turned away at last, untied, pulled out, turned left and sped up the five-mile pound towards Wigrams 3, Fosse 6, and the mighty Hatton 21.

CHAPTER X

Scrap Bullets and Bad News

Any boater would, I think, agree that the most pleasant form of boating is charging along the cut with an empty cross-strapped pair in dry sunny weather. There are no fears about snags waiting to get entangled in the prop. or snap the coupling bolts. The boats are skittish instead of sluggish. The speed is exciting instead of depressing. Worries are minimal. With us all was right with the world, and we were heading for the start of yet another trip which, though along a now well-known way, would quite certainly be unlike any trip done before.

Although we were enjoying all this, we could not shake off a sense of loneliness. The other pair were missing. That friendship, though quickly made, seemed real and in retrospect sadly short. Certainly it would never be renewed with the same intensity, for circumstances would not allow it. On the cut one never arrived, but was always coming from or going to somewhere. An arrival was not an ending but a temporary cessation of movement. We should meet the Phelps family again—for minutes as we passed in opposite directions, for hours, perhaps, of an evening in the same lay-by. But never, unless the odds were strangely in our favour, should we know them as a family and be with them through whatever experiences might come our way. There was something sad about the thought.

Tyseley smelt horrible, but all at the wharf were as happy and busy as usual. Pairs lined the hard. Colourful garments waved from bow hauling lines, as the breeze blew through the drying laundry, making it look as if the little ships were dressed with bunting. Men were polishing, women scrubbing, children everywhere playing and screaming. Diesels were throbbing, lorries hooting, cranes lifting and lowering. Some people were talking; others laughing; others cussing, looking miserable and dirty too. It was a scene of activity, of colour, of life on the cut.

It delighted me, and as boaters waved or called a welcome, I felt as if at last we belonged; had been slowly and gently accepted by this poor, proud, unknown little minority of people. Tyseley made me feel happy again.

Gay returned from the office with the news that we were to be loaded with scrap bullets and shells for delivery to Brentford —probably that afternoon. But they were not likely to finish the job, so if we liked we could go into Brum, and they would handle the boats. We never wanted to see Birmingham again; so Gay shopped locally and I worked on the log. John, as usual, was polishing the engine, dipping tanks, sweating up nuts, cleaning the mud-box on the end of the cooling water system. He was also changing batteries; taking the one from our cabin along to the charging rack, and bringing one from it as replacement. We used the time well, preparing the boats with care and optimism for that trip we were always going to make but never did—the fast trip without trouble, without any delaying incident.

The log reads:

Thursday	15.35 hrs.	Loading commenced.
	17.30 hrs.	Butty loaded.
Friday	09.00 hrs.	Loading M.B. commenced.
	11.10 hrs.	Loading completed.
	11.50 hrs.	Let go from Tyseley.
	17.20 hrs.	Top of Hatton 21.
	19.20 hrs.	Through Hatton.
	19.40 hrs.	Tied up top of Capes 2.

Analysis.	7 hrs. 50 mins.	21 miles.	26 locks.
Average.	2·7 m.p.h.		
Cargo.	Scrap bullets.	46 tons 8 cwt.	
Rate.	10/- per ton.		
Remarks.	Light load. Must try to do a quick trip to make up for this. Weather excellent. All in good trim. Hung our lovely plates, and now we look like boaters; aboard I mean. Did Hatton 21 in 2 hours, which suggests we almost *are* boaters.		

This gave the bones of it only. It was one of those days which any man who works with both his brain and his hands would recognize. Everything seemed determined to go well. All three of us fused into one smoothly-working team. There was little talk at locks—just action and fierce orders screamed at holiday-makers who would insist on standing just where one most needed space. I am afraid we were terribly rude to them, but it was largely for their benefit, and essentially for that of their children, who could so easily have been swept into the depths of the locks. One couple with no fewer than four brats amused me no end. 'Get back there. Move those kids out of it.' They looked hurt, and went sideways into the next place where I would be working. 'Not there. Back. Move yourselves *back*. Get to hell out of it.'

'What an insolent creature, a typical bargee,' the woman remarked loudly to her husband, and he, greatly aggrieved, called out, 'We've got as much right here as you; so don't be so rude'. Forthwith he marched his clan to the edge of the lock and sat himself on a wooden bollard. At this moment the butty swept into the lock. Gay jumped for the parapet, ran up the steps, holding a wet side strap, and saw the family right in her path. 'Out of the damned way. Hop it,' she bawled, and cast the rope through the air. It flicked above the man's head, and fell round the bollard. Never did anyone move more quickly. I might add that in seconds that rope had hundreds of pounds of strain on it as it slowed, and finally checked the movement of the boat and its cargo.

'Never have I met such rudeness.You'd think they required the whole place to themselves. She did that on purpose, George, I'm sure.'

'It's just an act, my dear. One might almost imagine they were in a hurry, whereas, as far as I can see, they just drift through the countryside like tired tortoises.'

'Ha, ha. You are funny, but how right. Melissa, come away from the edge darling. *Melissa*, did you hear me ask you to do something? You did. Well, obey.'

As we left towns behind, the locks were less crowded, but then came the fishermen. Some of them were quite cross with us, calling all kinds of abuse and even suggesting that we had no right to be moving on the water, or that at least we could have slowed down. On one occasion we whipped a fellow's rod right away from under his nose. I think he must have been asleep, bottom fishing, his rod resting in a cleft stick stuck into the edge of the bank. Our propeller seized upon the frail line and chewed it up. The reel screeched. The fisherman awoke and put his hand out to lift the rod and strike at this superb fish. Greatly to his surprise, the rod leapt forwards into the cut, and tore through the water like a thin torpedo right towards our motor-boat. Unfortunately it did not arrive, but continued its career about half-way between monkey and butty. There was nothing, with the best will in the world, that we could do about it until the next lock. The conversation, loudly bawled to be heard above the diesel's noise, went something like this:

'Stop, stop I say. You've got my rod.'

'I can't stop, Dad. Leastwise not here,' John called.

'Stop, you young bugger. It's stealing. That's what it is. Give me my rod back.'

'You come and get it, matey. Next lock. *Next lock.*'

'That's miles. I want it now. You bloody well stop.'

'Don't talk so daft. I'll leave it by the lock.'

'I'll report you, that I will. I wouldn't trust you. Just a bleedin' gipsy. You'll steal it, I know.'

Now this gipsy remark riled John, for there are no people alive whom boaters detest more than gipsies. Gipsies have been known to break into the cabins of narrow boats left moored in quiet country stretches, whilst their crews went shopping or for a pint at a near-by local.

'Go and stuff yourself, you silly old bugger.'

'What did you say?'

'Go and jump in the cut. Get your own rod.'

'I'll give you a damned good hiding when I catch up with you. Just you wait, youngster.'

'I'm real scared.'

After this John limbered up by turning about half-a-dozen somersaults over his tiller. Then, fists clenched, he performed more drill—a few smart arms-upwards-stretch, sideways-stretch, forwards-stretch; and finished, to my horror, by doing a handstand on the counter of the moving boat.

I think the fisherman must have been impressed, because, grumbling and cursing apart, he took no offensive physical action against our mate when we eventually arrived at the next lock.

Saturday's log reads:

05.00 hrs.	Rise.
07.00 hrs.	Let go from Capes 2.
18.00 hrs.	Tied up Buckby Bottom.

Analysis. 11.00 hrs. 26 miles. 38 locks.
Average. 2·3 m.p.h.
Remarks. Another grand day. Sunshine. All worked well. Could this be it?

What a day! These simple figures convey so little of the knowledge, care and physical effort entailed, or the possible mistakes. You fail to disengage the gears on a loaded boat, and it crashes through a lock gate and charges down a seven- or eight-feet step, and you are inundated by hundreds of thousands of gallons of water. You are slightly careless, and your boat, home and cargo disappear before your eyes to rest at the bottom of a filled lock. Or your great, heavy wooden rudder is lifted off its pintles. From the moment a gear is engaged the propeller, as if resenting its normal function, seeks diligently for something to pick up and skittishly wind about its blades. One moment it is your friend; the next your bitterest enemy.

Then there is the exertion—running up hundreds of steps, making thousands of turns with your windlass to raise paddles which an average untrained person probably could not move. Pushing and pulling balance beams, running between lock gates, jumping on to the top of the cabin, climbing up from it, heaving thick ropes, straining on thin ones, and quickly splicing them together after making only a small mistake. You sweep with the long butty tiller to turn a boat, which is ten times as long as it is wide, round a sharp bend, and then finely judge your countersteering when she tries not only to go round but to keep on going round.

Every moment of each hour you are working, watching that a hundred tiresome things, which can easily go wrong, are not allowed to. You can never relax, even when the locks are filling, and to the onlooker you are lazily leaning against a balance beam. A whole series of thoughts are passing through your mind. Is the for'ard fender of the motor-boat going to catch on the gate? Is the butty clear at the stern? That snatcher, did it move then? Is the motor in gear? Is the cooling water circulating? Are the Buckby cans filled? That side strap is frayed. Will it last until the evening? Did you make the range up?

Eleven hours of this, without a single mistake, is a good day's work. I said as much to John, who smiled and remarked, 'You get used to it in time. Anyway, you worry too much.'

'But I've got to balance the accounts. Time lost means money lost, old pal. But, admit, we all did well today?'

'Not bad.'

I should have known better than to have asked.

'Reckon Emma should get our last letter today, Captain. That was a smasher.'

'You liked it, did you? The great thing is that she likes it too.'

'She will. She thinks you're wonderful. "He writes such pretty things," she says. And I say, "I tell him, Emma. It's me that writes really." And she says, "You never thought up that bit about the flowers and me. That was real beautiful." And I says, "That? Oh, that was daft stuff." Then she gives me a hefty clout, and says, "No such thing, John Redknap. That's what a woman likes to hear." '

'You still think you want to marry her, John?' I asked.

'Oh sure. We'll get spliced one day I reckon.'

The next day was even better, for there were many fewer locks, and only one incident — which John and I thoroughly enjoyed but Gay did not. She was lock-wheeling at the time, riding along surveying the scenery, inquisitively looking over hedges and not looking where she was going. Above Bridge 90 the towpath had collapsed into the cut for some yards. It had broken right away from the hedge, leaving a wide hole. She rode right smack over the edge into it. Really it was as well that she landed in the cut, where she only got wet. This made the accident funny. Had she come down on the land it might have been serious.

Our figures for the day show how successful we were, and tell of our thirst when evening came, for we had reached Fenny—that little lock disliked by Gay but nevertheless placed outside the door of a pub. We tied up at five o'clock in the evening after only ten hours work.

Sunday.	05.00 hrs.	Rise.	
	10.00 hrs.	Away from Buckby Bottom.	
	12.15 hrs.	Speak Sister Mary at Stoke.	
	17.00 hrs.	Tied up Fenny.	
Analysis.	10.00 hrs.	34 miles.	9 locks.
Average.	3·4 m.p.h.		

In the pub, downing pints with ease and pleasure, we talked excitedly about the trip. It was going really well. So far it was the fastest ever. Certainly we had seventy-eight locks and fifty-four miles to go, but, hell, what was that?

We were playing darts when we heard the first rumble of thunder. A cool breeze invaded the bar. It was too cool. It was cold as death. Then the rain began; the breeze became a wind. And our cabin doors were wide open. We drank up and fled through the splashing, gale-driven rain to our homes. Safe inside, we listened to the great drops drumming on the timber roof; watched them drive into the cut and rebound. The surface of the water looked as if a thousand small fountains were rising from below. The storm rolled along from astern, mounting in noise, crashing and splitting its way across a yellow sky, now floodlit by sheet lightning, now pierced by brilliant flashes of forked, which seemed to dart down into the country behind us.

We had supper and turned in early, but it was impossible to sleep. The storm cracked away right above our heads with reports like ack-ack guns — sharp, ear-splitting, tremendous, almost overpowering in their magnificence. Nature's percussion played fortissimo, greater even than Beethoven or Wagner. I whistled pieces from the 'Pastoral' and thought about Brünnhilde, the Rhine and Götterdämmerung. The storm passed over, curved away, and came roaring back again from astern. It was a night of noise, dreams and fitful sleep.

At seven next morning we left Fenny. It was raining, but the countryside gave off a lovely scent of growing green things, and the air was wine. We climbed hard and fast through Leighton, up the Nag's Head 3, up Peter's 2, into the Marsworth Flight, past Rodney's pub, with a sigh, to the summit. John had been lock-wheeling, as I wanted to learn how to bring my boats up this crazy stretch without using the parapets as rudders. At the top the lock-keeper appeared at his door, stuck two fingers into his mouth, let go a tearing whistle and beckoned. John walked towards him. 'No,' he bellowed. 'Not you. Steerer Fern.'

I walked into his office.

'I've bad news for you, I'm afraid. For all of us in fact.'

'Oh well, what is it? I thought things were going too smoothly.'

'It's about the Bucks. There's been a bad accident . . . '

'Not Emma. Don't say it's Emma.'

'No, the kid's all right. Very shaken though. It's the old man.

He's in hospital in Uxbridge, broken to pieces. Little hope for him, I'm afraid.'

'Why, what happened?'

'The usual. Last evening. Just come up to Widewater when the storm broke. Silly old bugger was wearing rubber-soled shoes; hurrying, slipped on the lock-side. Nearly saved himself, Mrs Buck says; then let out a scream and fell with a crash on to the motor, and then down into the water between it and the lock-side.'

'God, poor devil! Not drowned then?'

'No. Somehow the women checked the butty, and got round to him, but couldn't lift him out. They dragged him to the side of the lock. One held him up while the other made a line fast to him. They heaved him along together, and pulled him ashore on the towpath.'

'What a terrible experience for them.'

'You know Widewater—miles from anywhere. Emma ran for help. Missis nursed her old man. He was out, of course. They tell me that when at last ambulance chaps arrived with a stretcher, the sight and sounds was like nothing you'd ever seen. Thunder, lightning, rain belting down, and Mrs Buck just sat there cradling her man's head in her lap, talking all the time to him, the water pouring off her in streams.'

'So there goes another of the old timers, I suppose.'

'No doubt. His ribs, pelvis and one leg are all broken, and with the time it took to get him into hospital he'll develop pneumonia for certain.'

'What do you want me to do? Tell John? Anything else?'

'No, that's the lot. The boats have been taken back to the depôt, load an' all. Don't know what will happen next.'

'I'll do that. Bye now.'

They both came up to me outside. 'What's happened? What's the matter? You look as white as a sheet.'

'It's bad news, I'm afraid. There's been an accident.'

'Not me folks? Not Emma?'

'No, John, they're all right. But Emma's father is in hospital.'

I told him some of the story only; then lit a much-needed cigarette. John kicked fiercely at a few stones; then turned to us and said, 'Let's be going, shall us?'

It was still raining, but now a kind of sad rain, with no joy and not even anger in it. We pushed on, toiled downwards through Berkhamsted and tied up in the lay-by below the town. Other boats were there, but the cut and ourselves were quiet. I made up our log. We had been on the move for 10½ hours, travelled twenty-three miles, and worked thirty-three locks at an average of 2·1 m.p.h. I slammed it shut, and threw it on to the shelf. It didn't seem to matter any more.

The next day was a twelve-hour slog through thirty-five locks. At 7.30 in the evening we tied up just above the depôt, having covered twenty-six miles. Gloom hung over the cut. We worked quietly. Others did the same. Even when we passed boats, the normal cheerful greetings became a nod or a 'How do?' Everyone was thinking about Albert Buck and his family. John and I walked past the dry dock and the great paint-shed to the lay-by, and up to the first steerer we met.

'What's the news?' I asked.

Simply and quietly he answered, 'He's gone on. Passed away in the night. His missis and Emma with him, but he never knew'd.'

The lay-by was still. Plenty of boats were in, but the hard was deserted and quiet. There were no battery radios playing and not a child in sight.

We returned to our pair. John walked along to the Buck's boats. The cabin doors were shut, and nobody was aboard. He came back and went down into his cabin.

At 8.45 a.m. on the Wednesday morning we winded in Brentford, and Gay hurried to report at the office while I made up our log. We sat around all that day, and were not unloaded until 3 o'clock in the afternoon of Thursday. Whereas Tyseley loaded the cargo in 3½ hours, Brentford took 5 hours to unload. Nevertheless it had been a good trip, and we had covered 133 miles and worked 169 locks at an average of 2·4 m.p.h.

CHAPTER XI

Two-Handed Again

As soon as our boats were emptied, Gay returned to the office, and asked if there were any orders for us. Or should we return to the lay-by at Bull's Bridge?

'Hold on a minute. I've got to phone the Bridge. I'll let you know as soon as possible.'

She came back, and we were sitting talking about the trip when we heard a gentle knocking on the cabin.

'Who is it?'

'Only me, John.'

'Oh, come on in. Come and sit down.'

'I've been wondering, Captain. Should I go to them now?'

'I don't want you to think I'm trying to hold you to these boats, but truly, if I were you, I should leave them alone and together for the present. We will find out about the funeral. Go to that, and perhaps you will be able to talk to Emma afterwards. Have the Bucks any folks on the land?'

'Yes, around Brentford here.'

'Well, possibly Mrs Buck will decide to pack in and go ashore. Anyway, John, my advice to you is: Don't go for a few days. But you are free to do just as you wish.'

'You know best, Captain, I'm sure. I'll do as you say. I'm going to work on me engine now.'

He left the cabin, and in a few moments we heard the metal doors of the engine-room clang as they were opened.

Pairs in the depôt lay-by were allotted cargoes on a rota system. On the Tuesday, when we had pulled in for the night, I had noticed that there were a fair number of boats waiting; and for a Number One, or rather a free-lance boater like myself, this was an unwelcome sight. Now we remained, day after day, in Brentford dock, waiting.

John, looking as uncomfortable as on the day he first called on us, went to Albert Buck's funeral, and returned shortly afterwards. He had talked to Emma, but found her strangely changed. She had no idea what her mother was going to do. Immediately after the funeral the Bucks returned to their boats, went below and shut the cabin doors.

The rest of the story I heard from Mr Newbury. I was called to the phone in the Brentford office.

'Steerer Fern?'

'Speaking.'

'Newbury here. I want to ask you a favour.'

'I know. You want young John.'

'Yes. How did you guess that?'

'I've been writing letters. Somehow felt sure this would happen. The old lady has decided to stay on the cut then?'

'Yes. She spent a day talking things over with her daughter; then walked in here and said to me, "Get us John Redknap. I'm staying on me boats if you've no objection." Could you spare him for a while until they get fixed up?'

'Of course. I'll send him up to them right away. Meanwhile you might look around for another third for me.'

'But he'll be back with you in a week or so.'

'I don't think he will. You'll see.'

'What makes you say that?'

'John and Emma are courting, that's what. And when do I get some orders?'

'Soon now. You're nearing the top of the rota. Well thanks. I'll tell them he'll be along. Goodbye.'

I walked slowly back to the boats feeling suddenly sad. Our lives had become strongly entwined with John's life. To us he was a great deal more than a third hand. Our master and my pupil was leaving us.

Before I reached the boats he called, 'Orders, Captain?'

'Yes, John. Orders—for you.'

'For *me*! What you mean?'

'Come into our cabin. I want to talk to you.'

He immediately looked as a loved dog looks when one scolds it. All life and vigour deserted him. Downcast, moving slowly, he crossed to our boats and came below.

'Now listen, John. The Bucks want you to go with them. Missis has decided to stay on the cut. They need a man to help them along. Emma would naturally think of you immediately. Mr Newbury asked me to release you and send you up to the Bridge as soon as possible.'

'But I can't go, Captain. I belong with you. Emma's all right, but her mother's tough. Besides, I can't be with two women.'

'We don't want you to go, John, but these people need you. Now that her husband has gone, Mrs Buck will probably be different. She'll depend on you to a large extent. You'll be the captain, I don't doubt. Emma's moving in with her mother. You'll have the motor to yourself. You must go for a while at least. You can't let Emma down when she most needs you.'

'Suppose not. But I'll be back. Will you have me back?'

'Of course, stupid. We'll go along two-handed for a while, and you let us know how you're going on. And write your own letters. You can do that now. And keep reading books. Don't go and forget all I have taught you.'

'I don't know what me dad will say.'

'He'll be proud of you. You left him a kid. Now you'll be doing a man's job, accepting responsibility, probably as a captain. That's not bad in a few months.'

'I'll go then. But I'll be back as soon as I can. Don't know how you'll get along without me. It'll slow you down something awful.'

'We'll do our best, and certainly we shall miss you. But I feel you should go.'

'Are all your clothes clean and dry, John?' Gay asked.

'Yes, Missis.'

'Don't worry about your cabin. I'll straighten it.'

'Thanks, Missis. I'll be going then.' He rose, and climbed the steps to the cockpit slowly, all spring gone out of him.

'Give us a call when you see a pair going up,' I said.

'I'll do that.'

Left alone, we didn't speak of him. Both of us, I think, purposely avoided the subject. At last we heard the sound of a diesel engine starting up, looked out and saw a pair backing into Lock 100 to be gauged. John called, 'I'll be off then'.

'Coming, John.'

We walked with him to the pair. He asked the steerer for a lift up to the Bridge. He went aboard, and we passed over his worldly possessions—a battered fibre suitcase lashed with cord, an old khaki pack and a kitbag. The diesel's revolutions rose. 'Bye, John. God bless. And don't forget what I've taught you about wearing damp clothes. Look after yourself.' Gay shook his hand, turned quickly and walked away. He extended his great fist to me. We shook. I slipped him a couple of pounds, and called, 'Promise me you'll buy a good dictionary with some of that, and keep on reading and writing.'

'I promise, Captain, and thank you for all you teached me'; then, as a quick afterthought and with a smile, 'But I'll be back.'

The pair drew away. He stood balanced on the three-inch gun'ale around the motor's cabin, not even holding on, and waved. We looked towards him until he disappeared around the first bend, still waving.

* * * *

We were loaded the next morning with 50 tons of Australian flour in bags for delivery to the Ministry of Food Buffer Depôt at Tring. This was an excellent bit of luck, for these short trips were much more profitable. For the 133-mile trip with bullets the rate was ten shillings. For this trip, of only 35 miles, we received seven shillings a ton. The Tyseley run took 54 hours; this only 16.

It was a strange feeling to be two-handed again, but it amused us to realize how much more efficient we had become. Now, even the boats seemed to co-operate with us, whereas previously it had been one long battle against them. We had fifty-five locks to work on this short haul, and it was pretty obvious that our speed was slowed seriously by the absence of a lock-wheeler. The whole character of our boating was changed. Gone was the pleasure of varying our duties—butty-steering, on the motor, on a bicycle or ambling about the boats, cleaning the brass, or splicing a rope as one sat on the fore-deck in the sunshine. Whereas with three-handed boating we hurried, but won an occasional breather, now we went like mad without any rest.

We left Brentford on a Tuesday, and were back in the lay-by at Southall by Friday evening, having earned £17 10s.

'Goodness,' Gay exclaimed. 'A few more like that, and we'd begin to make some money.'

'I wonder how John is getting on,' I remarked.

'Funny you should have said that then. I was thinking of him too. In fact I always am. I still lay three places at the table, and then remember. I make tea for three, and wonder why he is late for a meal.'

'I know exactly what you mean. I hear the quietness of the other boat, wonder what he can be doing, and remember also. We are in a difficult position now, for I'm sure he will never come back. Yet I don't like to spread word along the cut that we are looking for another hand. How long we shall be forced to go two-handed I don't know. I should hate him to feel that we had hurried to replace him even before he had decided not to come back to us.'

'Oh well. Not to worry, eh?' Then once more she came out with it. 'I see no ships, only bloody hardships.'

We were lucky again with our next trip, or rather we thought so at first. We were ordered to carry 25 tons of short lengths of beech wood from Brentford to Fenny Stratford. This was for delivery to a firm which made brushes, and the timber was packed in large hessian sacks. The loading took under four hours and the journey twenty-five hours, but we arrived on a Friday evening. At the office we were told we should have to wait until Monday to be unloaded. We had worked like mad to get there, hoping that they would unload us on the Saturday, and then we could push on up-country towards the coalfields on Sunday. We consoled ourselves with the thought that our bulky 25 tons of cargo was paid for at the rate of eleven shillings a ton and estimated at 40 tons. We should receive £22 for the trip.

This consolation began to fade on the Monday, when we were asked to bring our boats into a particular length for unloading, but discovered that, try as we might, we could not get nearer than five feet from the hard because of silting. As a result, by 4.30 p.m. on Monday, when they retired from the job, the motor was only half emptied. We finally left Fenny at 11 on Tuesday morning.

Our orders were to run empty to Hawkesbury for coal. So away we went flat out along the seventeen miles to Stoke Bruerne, where the lock-keeper called us into his office saying, 'You're to phone the depôt, mate.'

I phoned, and was told that no boats were wanted at Hawkesbury, and I should return to Southall. We winded and tied up in Fenny again that night. We were back where we had started ten hours before, having worked ten locks and travelled thirty-five miles! We were displeased.

A letter from John arrived sooner than we had expected. I won't quote it here, because, although it was so funny, I could imagine the toil and time it had cost him. It was both laughable and brave. The gist was that he commanded the pair, that, going back through Widewater, the women had broken down, that he was comfortable, but not happy, because Emma was so quiet and sad. The engine, he said, was a bugger and not like 'ours', and now he was waiting for coal at Baddesley. There was nothing definite in the letter about his future intentions, so on we plodded by ourselves.

We worked our way down the tortuous Marsworth Flight one evening in August, and headed for the lay-by. A few pairs were already tied up, and, while I was deciding where to pull in, I saw a whole family waving. Then a young woman and a small boy came running towards us. We had breasted-up. I said to Gay, 'Look who's here—Violet and Kim. The Phelpses are in the lay-by.'

'Oh, how lovely.' Then to Violet she called, 'Hullo, Vi. Hullo Kim. How are you?'

'Oh Gay, what fun. Come in behind us. Dad will take your lines. Two-handed again then? We passed John and Emma!' Violet ran along the towpath beside us talking incessantly, spilling out news of where they had been and whom they had seen.

I eased the boats into the bank. Jim made fast for'ard; Sarah and Violet aft. Kim stood looking at us, twisting and playing with his fingers. He was no longer the pale little boy we had known, but a bronzed, tough-looking kid, a miniature version of Jim and very like him.

'How do, Captain. 'Tis good to see you again.' We shook hands, and Sarah, watching, suddenly decided that she should also.

'And Kim?' I asked. 'How's this boy? He looks well enough.'

'He's been fine, thank you, Captain.' Sarah smiled at me, and threw an arm round her son, who shook himself free immediately, being quite unable to put up with such a display of affection in public. 'In fact he never looked back. Just eats and eats. You're some doctor, we decided.'

We talked for a few minutes; then Sarah, Violet and Gay went aboard our butty, while Kim and I cleaned the boats and arranged everything according to custom. Phelps had returned to his pair.

When we had finished our duties, Kim sat on our cabin roof and I on the butty counter. The boy told me of all the places and incidents he had recently seen. Soon I noticed Phelps walking towards us carrying a most beautifully painted and brand-new Buckby water-can. It was perfect, every piece of it covered with blue, green, yellow, black, red and white paint. The top was a mass of flowers. The body was divided into four bands, two narrow, two wide. Here was the Rhineland-type castle, the bridge over a blue stream; there tall trees in a fenced meadow. Above was a narrow band of flowers; above that the clustered roses. It was superb, traditional, gay.

'How do you like it?' he asked, as he placed it on my cabin roof and spun it to show off all the pictures.

'Wonderful, a real beauty. Whoever painted that?'

'I did o' course. My dad teached me, same as his dad teached him. I painted all our dippers and cans, and many more besides. I like painting pretty things like this. Anyway, you can stow that old British Waterways thing of yours out of sight, as this is for you with our best respects.'

'No, Jim. You can't do that. Damn it, man, already you have given us those wonderful plates. I can't keep taking these gifts from you.'

'It's for you and your Missis, and that's all there is to be said.'

'Gay, come out and look at this.'

All the women crowded into the cockpit. I jumped for the towpath. 'Jim, here, has painted that for our boats. Isn't it lovely?'

She stood for a few seconds looking at the can, Sarah and Violet watching her. Then quite slowly she said, 'That can for us? You painted it, Jim?'

'Yep. 'Tis for you. Time an' all you had a proper can on your boats, Missis.'

'Oh thank you, Jim. But it's too lovely to use. It might get damaged.'

'It will take you some time to knock all the paint off it. That I'll be bound. Then I'll paint her again.'

The Phelpses had eaten; so, while we washed, Kim was put to

bed. Then we all walked—Jim and Gay arm-in-arm ahead, myself with Sarah on one side and Violet on the other—to the 'Red Lion' to celebrate our reunion and christen the can. Rodney was in his usual good form, and the pub was busy. The Buckby can was filled with gallons of best bitter, and we stood a drink to everyone who was consuming that excellent brew. The evening was full of laughter, happiness, music and singing. For us to be with the Phelpses again was a real pleasure, and I said as much to Jim, who took a long swig from his tankard, lowered it and replied, 'For us too, matey. We as works the cut come to care for some things a great deal. Friendship and a helping hand like what you gave us. Good weather. A good engine in painted boats. And an evening like this. Haven't had one for a long time. Let me fill your glass up.'

He poured mine from the can, topped up his own, and walked round the bar topping up other people's. Then he came back, raised his tankard and said, 'Well, here's to old Albert Buck. God bless him. As tough an old runt as ever steered a pair. I'll miss him. One of the real old timers.'

We raised our mugs, and together chimed, 'Albert Buck, God bless him'. And not another word of the tragedy was spoken.

He asked me what we were doing about finding another third hand. I explained the difficulty. 'Let me know as soon as you decide to take another boy. I found you John. I'll find you another soon enough,' he said.

We parted on the towpath after much talking. Again we thanked Jim for the can, and, waving to one another, stepped aboard our boats and went home.

About a week later we passed John and the Bucks in the long pound near Weedon. The calling, waving and shrieking were tremendous. John turned somersaults, did a few hand-stands and generally expressed his pleasure at the meeting. Emma was smiling again, and after the summer sunshine she looked even darker skinned, even prettier. Mrs Buck waved once; then rested on her tiller. She looked sad and frail, a striking contrast with the lively creatures about her.

Soon after this meeting I first noticed among the many chalkings on the balance beams the letters EB over JR, and I wondered if it was their way of telling me that they were going to pair up. John knew I would understand the significance of the letters.

Perhaps he felt that this was the easiest way to break the news.

We tied up earlier than usual about two days after this meeting. We were tired after toiling down through Berkhamsted and Watford, and agreed to have an early night. Our boats were cleaned and tidied as usual. We were smoking, lying full-length on the roof of the butty, enjoying the evening sun and listening to the sounds of the countryside. A distant pair throbbed their way towards the lock by which we were moored. The lower gates were open, ready for them. When they arrived we sat up, saw it was the Hones and decided to go to help them through. At the downhill end, the balance beams of a lock are moved in an arc across a small area of land which has to be built up to the level of the uphill end. This rise is sometimes made by a slope, but sometimes it is vertical, and contained by brick or stone walling.

Gay moved down one side of the lock, I the other. The pair glided sweetly into the compartment. Mrs Hone came running up the steps with her side strap. I called out, 'Carry on. We'll close the gates.' They moved quickly to the far end, and began raising the paddles. I looked across the lock, and saw Gay pulling the gate shut, and wondered why on earth she was doing it not only the hard but the wrong way. She should, like myself, have been leaning against it. The gates banged together, and, thinking no more for the moment of Gay, I ambled up to give Hone the welcome news of a good road ahead of him, for we had just come down and not seen a pair since Salters. We talked as the lock filled. Then he stepped on to his counter and opened the throttle, and away they went.

I looked round. Gay was nowhere to be seen. I called, and a distant voice answered, 'I'm here. I'm all right.'

'Where are you?'

'Below the balance beam. I fell over the wall.'

I charged across the lock gates, tore down the stone stairs and found her lying on the ground about nine feet below where she had been standing a few minutes previously. Later, I asked how she had come to do such a thing. She explained that being relaxed, in no hurry, she had pulled the beam towards her, and, when the gates had closed, had stepped backwards to gain room to walk around the end of the thing, forgetting about the drop behind her.

I tried to raise her into a sitting position, but she let out a scream. 'Don't move me. Not yet. I'll be all right. I landed on my tail. Leave me awhile.'

'Move your legs, Gay. Come on. This one. Move it.'

It moved. I touched the other. 'Now this. Come on.' That moved also. 'No pain in them?'

'No, they're all right. It's only my spine, at the base, where it hurts.'

'Try sitting up. That's it. Arms O.K.? Waggle your head. Good. I think you are all in one piece. Here, smoke this.'

Later I took her back to the butty, but it was a slow business getting her down inside and on to the bed. Remembering my first-aid lessons, I immediately made strong sweet tea, and there she stayed until next morning, when she declared that all was well again. But obviously it was not. Sudden movements, bending, all her weight on one foot—these hurt still. We agreed to stay tied up for the day.

Next morning we continued our journey, crawling downwards through Coppermill and Denham towards Lock 88 at Uxbridge. Gay stayed on the boats. I did all the lock work. Our progress was slow, but Brentford was not far away. At Cowley, while the lock was slowly emptying, I filled our Buckby can at the tap nearby. The lock-keeper asked why I was working alone. I told him. 'You open the gate your side,' he said. 'I'll go round and open the other for you.'

'Thanks,' I replied, leant downwards, grabbed the can and jumped to the cabin roof.

I heard the bang in my ears, heard singing noises start, felt my arms stiffen. Stars shot about before my eyes. I crawled off the cabin on to the counter, and somehow managed to hitch the snatcher on to the dolly. Slowly we crawled from Cowley into the long pound which ended at Norwood Locks. I knew exactly what had happened, because this was not the first time. Somehow that last jump must have been a bad one. Probably the heavy can in one hand had not helped. I had jolted the three damaged bones in my neck out of position. My shoulders were hunched. I could look neither to right nor left. The ends of my fingers tingled with pins and needles and were without other feelings.

Now we were in a mess, with two loaded boats and two crocks

to work them. I felt sure I could carry on slowly, doing everything except winding up the paddles. This would certainly be too much, but Brentford was now only about nine miles distant, and there were a decent crowd of fellows on the Norwood Flight. We'd make it, somehow. From Brentford it was no distance to our home in Richmond, or to Queen Mary's at Roehampton. I smiled at the memory of the doctor there, and wagered with myself that his first words would be' What, you again?'

Whether Gay had noticed my climb from the roof to the counter or not I didn't know, but quite certainly she would immediately spot my trouble at Norwood. When this business happened, apart from stiffening up, I looked crooked, and could do nothing to hide it.

We ploughed ahead. Steering was not too difficult. As we neared Norwood I decided to tell the keeper what had happened, and ask him to work us down the flight. He was a good fellow, and his jacket bore the ribbons of service in two theatres of war. He, I felt sure, would help us.

The first lock was open, and Jack leant on the beam waiting for us. I took the boats in at a crawl. Gay tossed her side strap towards him and called, 'Fix it for me, Jack. I'm in trouble.' I had stepped ashore. She took one look at me and bellowed, 'Not you, *too*?'

'Yes, I'm afraid so. At Cowley. Must have made a bad jump. Not to worry. We're nearly there, and as soon as we are unloaded we will go to see our respective doctors. Cheer up. We're still alive.'

Jack, the old devil, laughed heartily, and passed some coarse remark about 'hamateurs'. Then, with his mate helping, he cheerfully worked us down the flight. At the bottom he yelled, ' 'Arry will come and get you through the other two. 'Ave a good rest in 'orspital, mate. And you'd better buy yourself a rubber cushi'n to fit inside your bags, me dear.'

Gay was rude to him. He loved it, chuckled, waved to her, and began the long walk back to the top of his flight.

Harry did his stuff in great form, and admitted to me that, but for his wife and kid, he would be a steerer. There was nothing he liked more than a ride on the cut.

Our old friend in the office at Brentford laughed when I walked in. He asked, 'You got a stiff neck then?'

'Yes. When can you unload us? I'm in a bit of a hurry.'

'You, you're always in a hurry. Now let's see. Um, hold on a minute while I go and talk to Bert.'

They unloaded us next day, and from the office I received permission to tie the boats up in a quiet spot. We clipped padlocks on the cabin doors and went ashore.

CHAPTER XII

The Last Trip

I was sitting in the same old room, waiting as usual. The door opened. He came in, looked at me, and loudly said, 'What, you again?' I laughed. We shook hands—gently.

'What do you find to laugh at?'

I told him of my wager with myself. 'Come over here. Lie down on that, and relax.' He felt along my neck. 'How did you do it this time?'

I told him the truth. He exploded. 'Working boats! Are you mad? How often do I have to tell you not to do these stupid things? Monkeying about in boats on a canal! Give it up, you damned fool.'

We talked awhile. I tried to explain a few things to him. I spoke of 'we'.

'We? Who was with you?'

'Gay. You remember her—my wife.'

'You took her on this mad venture? She must be crazy too. How is the lovely lady?'

I told him about her accident. He rubbed his chin; then said coldly, 'She did, uh? I might have guessed it. Not only are you doing your best to kill yourself but you are trying to kill her too. You're both mad.'

Before I left the hospital he saw me again. 'How do you feel now?'

'Oh fine. It's great to be free again. Thank you for what you have done.'

'For the last time I want to warn . . . '

He talked non-stop for about ten minutes—about manipulations, cervical vertebrae and bloody fools. He finally threatened me with exposure to the Army medical authorities if I did not promise him forthwith to stop working boats. I promised. He then talked for ten more minutes about all the horrors which could befall me. I fled, feeling grateful, but sad at the thought that we might have to relinquish the cut. My promise worried me. I decided to talk the whole matter over with Gay.

After many hours' conversation, which at times became quite heated, we came to the conclusion that we should give up the life and try something less physically exacting but in which we would be our own masters. There followed many visits to Waterways officials to explain our retirement and offer our thanks for all their help. We had a final meeting with our friend in the Executive, during which we made a considered statement concerning the ills of the canal system and suggested some remedies. He thanked us for all the reports we had sent to him, and promised us that, to the limit of his resources, action would be taken. He expressed sorrow at losing us, and, after leaving him, we felt that we had in some measure repaid the cut for all the pleasure it had given us.

We returned to Brentford about a week after leaving it. Gay had recovered her agility, but said, 'It still hurts where my tail should be'. I felt perfectly fit, and looked quite normal again. This was the snag of my disabilities. I always had been outstandingly strong. I looked tough and enjoyed physical exertion. Yet I had three damaged bones in the left shoulder and three more in the neck, and the chance of something going wrong was more than possible. It was likely.

We opened the door of our cabin and looked in, and there was home. Everything was in order. Only the wild flowers were dead in the wall-vase. Yet in the interval since we had left we had decided to give this home up for ever. Frankly it seemed impossible. This was our world. Here was almost everything we possessed. Certainly here were all the things we loved. The sun shone on our fragile plates, our colourful Buckby can, on the old kettle who had so often nearly saved our lives. I could swear he was smiling with pleasure to see us back, and longing to feel the heat of the range warming his broad bottom.

Sentimental bosh? To some perhaps—probably to those who have not striven, as we had, to obtain the commonplace things of life; neither battled for them, nor experienced the joy of gifts in remembrance of adversity shared.

We changed quietly into our working clothes.

'Ready?'

'Yes.'

We moved to the engine-room. I turned on taps and looked around. All was in order. I swung the great handle.

'Now!'

She fired first time, picked up her rhythm slowly, took a hold of herself and ran smoothly at last.

'Look at our brass,' Gay said. 'It's filthy. We can't go back to the depôt like that.'

'Certainly not. You do the brass. I'll wash the boats down.'

Nobody came to talk to us because we were tied up far from other boats, but we looked down towards the heart of the dock.

'The Blossoms are in,' she said.

'And Hill, there, look.'

'They're loading grain. For Leicester, perhaps.'

'You finished, Gay?'

'Yes, that's better. I reckon John would pass that.'

'Let's get to hell out of here. The place depresses me.'

'Don't say it. Cast off, and get a bloody move on.' She laughed, and went down into the butty cabin.

We worked 99 and 98 as if we were off for orders. We made no mistake, but went smoothly and quickly. Then came Norwood Flight, with Jack and Harry.

'Been on yer 'olidays then?' Harry asked.

'Good to see you back, mate. All fit now?' Jack said.

'Yes, all fit, thanks. Come on, come on, open those paddles. We haven't got all day. Get weaving,' I quipped.

'Listen to 'im talkin'. Same as ever, 'arry, 'e is. No bleedin' peace now 'e's back. Go on then. Get to 'ell aht of it.'

'Thanks, Jack. Thanks, Harry. Be seeing you,' Gay called.

'Bye, Missis. 'Ave a care now and keep that cushin blowed up. Cor, fancy falling on yer arse off a lock. Just fancy that, I ask you.'

Their voices faded. The revs. jumped. We cut along towards the depôt. The pair were alive, moving buoyantly through laughing, splashing water—boats unleashed and rearing to go.

We passed the lay-by and waved to boaters who called and waved to us. Down went the revs. Out came the gear, as, first the paint-shed, then the dry dock, slowly moved from sight. We pulled in along the hard above the sheds, for here it would be easier to unload our gear. We could bring the car nearer to the boats, and we might be spared the questions of our friends.

It took two journeys to clear our belongings. As we worked, all life and personality drained from our cabins, until at last, empty, they became just wooden boxes, and our pair died before our eyes. The sadness of the task was almost unendurable. We were killing friends which had housed, warmed and protected us whenever we had had need of them. Towards the finish we hurried, in complete silence, to leave them. I took one final look as we walked away. Straps, Buckby cans, shafts and mops were gone. The brass of the extra cabin's porthole shone as though wet with tears. I saw her number, 229; then, in bold lettering, 'British Waterways', and finally, towards the stern, 'Bawtry'. Beyond, the motor-boat was hidden, and there was nothing to see of her except the black chimney with its three brass bands.

We moved towards Mr Newbury's office to say goodbye and thank him. He was on the phone. He pointed towards two chairs, and said, 'Hold on a minute'.

The only steerer in the lay-by whom we knew well enough to take into our confidence was Herbert Chitty. To him we explained the reason for our sudden departure, and we gave him messages for John, Emma, the Phelpses and a few others. Then we turned about and walked swiftly to the car.

* * * *

All that was years ago, yet today Gay and I can bring it all flooding back to our memories with a word. A strap for us was never made of leather. A boater is not a hat. A can is not a container holding a pasteurized amber liquid called beer, but a thing of beauty covered with traditional designs in brilliant paints. A cut remains a strip of water, and a lock is something you curse if it is closed against you and love if it is wide open.

We can still remember those stretches through cuttings and woods, along low meadows where the cattle trod down the banks and the cut invaded the pastures. We wonder about the boaters; how many of the old steerers are still alive, how many of those noisy kids are steerers now.

John married his Emma twelve years ago, soon after her frail old mother died. He told us that Mrs Buck hardly smiled again after Albert Buck's death; just worked her boat and faded away.

It was about five years ago that we went in search of them, and travelled miles of the cut until we found them at Braunston. Neither of us is likely to forget their faces when they came, two-handed, up to the bottom of the flight, and found the lock set fair by an elderly couple, comparatively smartly dressed, who knew how to work the paddles and carried their own windlasses. They had a six-years-old son, dark-skinned and handsome like his mother. They talked in the early days of their marriage of leaving the cut, but trip followed trip and they were happy. They had their own home, and gradually they forgot the idea.

The Phelpses are boating still, with Kim steering the motor. Violet married a docker, who works in Brentford Basin. He is a good fellow, and the family have great reunion parties whenever the boats come down for loading. As soon as his holidays arrive, he and Vi pack, rush up the cut and find the Phelpses, and Violet reaches for a tiller.

In retrospect I thank the fates for that chance meeting at 'Fishery Inn'. Perhaps our bodies suffered from our experiences on the cut, but our minds won a store of happy, fascinating memories. Certainly the venture healed my mind, and forever changed my outlook both upon myself and others. After it I remained self-employed and busied myself at creative tasks, and now I sit in my own home in sight of the water, which I always loved so much. I am surrounded by a number of things which mean little to many who see them — things like two hand-painted side-plates, a Buckby can—which an artist acquaintance described as 'barbarous, dear fellow. The man who painted this was without feelings or taste of any kind'—and a couple of crossed windlasses, which are regularly cleaned with emery-paper.

If either of us calls the other and complains of being kept waiting, the answer is simply, 'Hold on a minute'. And immediately annoyance is expelled by laughter.

GLOSSARY

BALANCE BEAM Heavy timber arm projecting from a lock gate. Used both to balance the gate, and to open or close it when the boater leans against it.

BERKO Boater's name for Berkhamsted.

BOW HAULING TOW-LINE A long cotton rope used when a pair are passing through a flight of narrow locks which contain only one boat at a time. The powered boat goes ahead. The butty boat is hauled through by the crew, who use this line attached either to the mast or stud on the bows of the butty.

BREASTING-UP Allowing the butty boat to come up alongside the monkey boat; then fixing straps from the bows and stern of one to the other.

BRIDGE HOLE Channel beneath the narrow humpbacked bridges. The water here is generally further restricted by the presence of the towpath.

BUCKBY CAN Large painted can for water storage. Carried on cabin trunk.

BUTTY BOAT A narrow boat which is not powered but towed. One of a pair.

BUTTY, TO Accompany one another, sharing work on locks.

CRATCH Shaped timber and tarpaulin covering at fore end of hold.

CUT Descriptive and sole name for canal, used by all who work upon it.

DIPPER Large cup-shaped metal vessel with handle, used as wash-bowl.

FENDERS Woven rope protectors. One on bow, one round the counter of the motor-boat.

FLIGHT A series of locks separated by short pounds.

JOSHERS Boatman's name for craft of the Joshua Fellows Morton and Clayton Carrying Company.

LEGGING Old-time method of working boats through tunnels which have no towpaths. The horses walked across the route, sometimes led, often alone. The boaters lay on their backs on long boards or 'wings' extending outwards from both sides of the fore deck, and pushed the boats along with their feet.

LENGTHMAN Employee of Waterways whose task is to maintain a 'length' of canal.

LOCK-WHEELING Moving on a bicycle from lock to lock and opening them for one's boats.

MAFAS Boater's name for Marsworth.

MONKEY BOAT A power-driven narrow boat.

NARROW BOAT A craft of wood or steel approximately 70 feet by 7 feet. Also called a 'long boat'.

NUMBER ONE A captain who owns his pair of boats.

PADDLE Wooden door which can be raised to admit, or lowered to exclude or retain, water in a lock.

PARKS, THE Lengths by Cassiobury Park, Watford.

POUND Stretch of canal between locks.

ROAD The route of the canal from pound to pound.

SIDE CLOTHS Tarpaulins folded and attached to gunwales.

SNATCHER A short length of thick manilla tow-rope. About 12 feet.

SNUBBER Long thick manilla tow-rope. About a boat's length or 70 feet.

STAIRCASE A series of locks in which the top gate of one is the bottom gate of another. Locks not separated by pounds.

STRAPS Ropes attached one to each side of a butty boat for'ard of the steering position. Used to check the forward movement of the boat at entrances or in locks. The word also used generally for short lengths of rope—cross straps, side straps, downhill strap employed to hold a butty boat back in a lock until the power-boat steerer is in position to take hold of the snatcher or snubber.

TOP CLOTHS Black tarpaulins used to cover hold.

WIND, TO To turn narrow boats round.

WINDING PLACE OR HOLE A wide area where a narrow boat can be turned around.

WINDLASS L-shaped metal crank to raise and lower lock paddles.

INDEX

(to pages 17 – 184 and plates only)
Plate numbers are shown in bold.

The following pages provide
details of some other books from

M & M BALDWIN

publishers and booksellers
specialising in inland waterways,
transport and industrial history

24 High Street
CLEOBURY MORTIMER
Nr Kidderminster
Worcs DY14 8BY
Tel: 0299 270110

Prices and availability are correct at the time of publication, but may be altered without notice.

In addition to our specialist publishing activities, we also run a bookshop stocked with a considerable range of out-of-print books on transport and industrial history (as well as general secondhand books). Our shop is open on Wednesdays 2–6, Fridays 10–6 (Easter to October), Saturdays 10–6, and at other times by appointment. We issue catalogues from time to time; if you would like your name to be added to our mailing list, please send an A5 stamped addressed envelope, and specify your interests.

IDLE WOMEN

In 1944, SUSAN WOOLFITT joined a Ministry of War Transport scheme to work on England's canals. In her book, she provides a lively and fascinating account of work on the canals during the second World War. This new edition is illustrated with contemporary photographs, showing life and work on the canals forty years ago.

The book is 8¾″ by 5¾″, is bound in real cloth with a two-colour dustwrapper, and has 223 pages and 18 photographs.

Price: £11.50 (post extra).

TOM ROLT AND THE CRESSY YEARS

IAN MACKERSEY unfolds the story of Rolt's involvement with the waterways, with Cressy, and with the Inland Waterways Association. Using unpublished information and photographs, Mackersey recreates the canal world of this famous industrial and transport historian.

'. . . the first time that the early history of the Association has been spelt out . . . extremely well-written . . .' *IWA Waterways*

'. . . a moving book, well-written by an author who clearly has sympathy with and sincerity in his subject . . .' *Newcomen Society Bulletin*

The book is 8¼″ by 5¾″, has 103 pages, 34 photographs and an index, and is bound in 3-colour card covers.

Price: £4.50 (post extra).

MAIDENS' TRIP

During the last war, the canals experienced such a revival of trade that women were recruited to crew the boats. One of these was 20-year old EMMA SMITH, who later wove her adventures into a fascinating book (which even inspired a TV series) bubbling with youth, yet providing an insight into the now-vanished world of narrow-boats and the families who worked them.

The book is 8½″ by 5½″, has 224 pages, and is bound in coloured card covers.

Price £5.50 (post extra).

BY LOCK & POUND

40 years ago, VIVIAN BIRD decided to travel by working boat from Birmingham to the estuaries of the Thames, Humber, Severn and Mersey. Some of his trips were by narrow boat, others on larger craft. They included a trip on the Severn with 130 tons of cheese; to Stanlow in tank boats; Nottingham to Hull on a tug, and a Birmingham cruise for the BBC. Throughout, he kept an eye open for details of craft operation, and recorded much useful information on cargoes and working practices.

The book is 8¾″ × 5½″, has 208 pages, 27 photos, 9 maps, and an index, and is hardbound with a full-colour dustwrapper.

Price £12.95 (post extra).

CANALS – A NEW LOOK

In 1984, Charles Hadfield, doyen of canal historians, celebrated his 75th birthday. As a tribute MARK BALDWIN and TONY BURTON edited this book, which contains chapters by seven canal experts, whose subjects range from push-tows to pleasure boating. Also included is the most extensive British canal bibliography ever published, describing 700 pre-1951 books and booklets.

Published by Phillimore, but we have acquired the entire unsold stock, and are offering it at well below the original price. 10″ by 7½″, 208 pages, 64 illns. Hardbound, full-colour dustwrapper.

Price: £9.50 (post extra).

VOYAGE IN A BOWLER HAT

In 1958, HUGH MALET cruised across the British Isles, from Ipswich to Waterford, via London, Ellesmere Port, Dublin, and Limerick. His account of the journey is memorable for its entertaining style, and for the view it provides of the waterway scene over thirty years ago, when canal cruising was still comparatively rare. No more extensive waterway trip in the British Isles has ever been described in print.

The book is 8½″ by 5½″, has 267 pages, 31 photographs, 3 maps and an index, and is bound in 2-colour card covers.

Price: £6.00 (post extra).

WILLIAM JESSOP, ENGINEER

This authoritative book, by CHARLES HADFIELD and Professor SKEMPTON, presents the only detailed biography of a remarkable engineer. His work embraced major docks (West India, Bristol Floating Harbour, etc), canals (Cromford, Grand Junction, Rochdale, Barnsley, Grand Canal of Ireland, Caledonian, etc), the River Trent Navigation, land drainage (Holderness, Isle of Axholme, etc), and several early railways (Surrey Iron, Kilmarnock and Troon). The authors demonstrate conclusively that Jessop was the leading engineer of his day.

'... meticulously detailed and referenced ... has all the hall-marks of confident scholarship and will certainly remain a standard work of reference for years to come.'
Technology & Culture

' At last the real creator of the British inland navigation system is acknowledged ... undoubtedly Jessop was this country's pre-eminent waterways engineer.' *Waterways World*

The book was published by David & Charles, but we have acquired the entire unsold stock. It is 8½" by 5½", has 315 pages, 22 photographs, 24 text maps and diagrams, and an index. It is hard bound, and has a pictorial dustwrapper.

Price: £10.00 (post extra).

AFLOAT IN AMERICA

A delightful book, which tells the story of the three months which CHARLES and ALICE MARY HADFIELD spent on their North American tour in 1978, clocking up about 5,000 miles by waterway.

Originally published by David & Charles at £4.50, this is a hardback of 160 pages with 32 photographs and maps.

Our special price: £2.50 (post extra).

HISTORICAL CANAL MAPS

In conjunction with Cartographics, we publish a series of authoritative maps compiled by leading canal cartographer, RICHARD DEAN. These show a wealth of historical detail not available elsewhere. They have been well received; a review of the map of Brimingham and the Black Country remarked: 'the clearest representation of the system I have ever seen'. Various areas have been covered; full details on request.